The Art of the Compliment

Also by Christie Matheson

Green Chic: Saving the Earth in Style
Wine Mondays: Simple Wine Pairings with Seasonal Menus
(with Frank McClelland)
The Confetti Cakes Cookbook (with Elisa Strauss)
Confetti Cakes for Kids (with Elisa Strauss)
Tea Party (with Tracy Stern)

The Art of the Compliment

Using Kind Words with Grace and Style

Christie Matheson

Skyhorse Publishing books may be purchased in bulk at special discounts for sales promotion, corporate gifts, fund-raising, or educational purposes. Special editions can also be created to specifications. For details, contact the Special Sales Department, Skyhorse Publishing, 555 Eighth Avenue, Suite 903, New York, NY 10018 or info@ skyhorsepublishing.com.

www.skyhorsepublishing.com

10 9 8 7 6 5 4 3 2 1

Library of Congress Cataloging-in-Publication Data

Matheson, Christie.
  The art of the compliment : using kind words with grace and style / Christie Matheson.
      p. cm.
  ISBN 978-1-60239-636-4
  1. Compliments. 2. Interpersonal relations. I. Title.
  P299.C593M38 2009
  158'.2--dc22

                                2009000195

Printed in China

To my friend Meg Power

(I know you resist taking compliments, but this time you have no choice. You are fabulous and I adore you, lady!)

"Everyone likes a compliment."
—Abraham Lincoln

Contents

Acknowledgments

Enormous thanks to Stacey Glick, the best agent and a fantastic friend. Thanks to Ann Treistman for the idea—and for being such an astute and stylish editor. Thanks also to LeAnna Weller Smith for the beautiful design, to production pros Abigail Gehring and Kathleen Go, to Skyhorse Publisher Tony Lyons, and to Skyhorse Associate Publisher Bill Wolfsthal.

And thank you to all those who were generous with their time and willing to share their compliment stories with me. You deserve the lovely compliments you told me about!

Introduction

"WOW . . . NICE CATCH!" Perhaps you suavely saved someone's wineglass from crashing to the floor. Maybe you just won the game for your company softball team by diving for a fly ball. Or possibly your new significant other's best friend is admiring what a hottie you are. Whatever inspired the compliment, chances are it made you feel fantastic.

As the American philosopher William James pointed out, "The deepest principle in human nature is the desire to be appreciated." That's just what a compliment does: lets someone know she is appreciated. And the desire to be valued never goes away.

Compliments are wonderful and powerful. They make us smile, can instantly transform our moods, and could turn a bad day (or week, or month) into a good one. The best compliments give us confidence and might even inspire us to greatness. Want to make someone feel cool, sexy, beautiful, smart, and successful? Give a compliment.

> Nothing makes people so worthy of compliments as receiving them. One is more delightful for being told one is delightful.
>
> —Katherine Gerould

Compliments can strengthen friendships, romantic relationships and family ties, and improve work situations. In fact, they make any interaction a little bit sweeter.

Erasmus wrote that flattery, when it stems from "ingenuous goodness of heart," is a powerful tool that "raises downcast spirits, comforts the sad, rouses the apathetic, stirs up the solid, cheers the sick, restrains the headstrong, brings lovers together, and keeps them united." It also "attracts children to pursue the study of letters, makes old men happy, and offers advice and counsel to princes." Whether or not you are advising any princes, remember that compliments make everyone "more agreeable and likable to himself, and this is the main ingredient in happiness."

That's a lot to accomplish with a few well-chosen and sincere words.

> I can live for two months
> on a good compliment.
>
> —Mark Twain

Better still, compliments don't cost a thing. So let's start paying more of them.

How do you give compliments with grace and style? Like any skill worth having, it may take a little practice. But soon it will start to feel really natural. Though it's not hard, following some basic guidelines can help you become a supremely skilled complimenter, and I'll help you navigate those rules here. Read on for encouragement, ideas, and tips for giving *and* receiving compliments. I think you'll find that mastering the art of the compliment is well worth your time.

P.S. I could end the introduction with a cute little compliment about your looks or your style, but I'm not going to do that. I can't see you right now, so would you believe me? What I do know, because you picked up this book, is that you're interested in learning more about compliments. And that means you're likely a caring and warm-hearted person who wants to make other people feel good.

The Art of the Compliment

A Brief History of Compliments

SOME HISTORIANS BELIEVE that the practice of paying compliments and flattering others is a hallmark of the beginning of civilized society. In 1714 the philosopher Bernard Mandeville commented that the earliest politicians "thoroughly examined all the strength and frailties of [human] nature, and, observing that none were either so savage as not to be charmed with praise, or so despicable as patiently to bear contempt, justly concluded that flattery must be the most powerful argument that could be used to human creatures . . . They extolled the excellency of our nature above other animals, and setting forth with unbounded praises the wonders of our sagacity and vastness of understanding, bestowed a thousand encomiums on the rationality of our souls, by the help of which we were capable of performing the most noble achievements."

Take those wild men sprung from rocks and trees—what power brought them into a civilized society if not flattery?

—Erasmus

History is filled with memorable and tangible examples of praise, from Roman monuments to Shakespeare's sonnets. The Egyptian pyramids, for example, were built as enormous, long-lasting tributes to royalty. History itself was first written and recorded as an exercise in praise of world rulers. Literature, too—especially poetry—began to flourish in the form of flattery to wealthy patrons. And those patrons loved it. After all, simply having someone compliment you as brilliant is nice, but having a poet write you an ode for all to read is sublime.

Poets penning complimentary words to their lovers dates back to at least the twelfth century, and smitten wooers have been giving compliments to the objects of their affection ever since. Shakespeare is a great source of inspiration for loverly compliments—he came up with such doozies as "Of the very instant that I saw you, did my heart fly at your service," and "I would not wish any companion in the world but you."

Even when creatures can't speak, they give praise. Look at chimpanzees, our closest ancestors. Chimps and other animals groom one another and mimic one another's actions—forms of flattery.

More people are flattered into virtue than bullied out of vice.

—Robert Smith Surtees

True, some praise (and historic monuments, love sonnets, and poetry) goes well beyond the sphere of the simple compliment and morphs into serious sucking up. I don't suggest you go that far, but the enduring nature of flattery demonstrates just how much people like it. And as long as you keep it simple and sincere, it's just a good compliment.

For centuries, great thinkers and leaders have understood and extolled the power of compliments. Abraham Lincoln was incredibly effective as a politician and president, in part because he rarely criticized and often complimented. Although it might seem counterintuitive not to criticize when you believe someone needs to change his or her behavior or tactics, praise can accomplish so much more.

One of the reasons British Prime Minister Benjamin Disraeli held so much sway with Queen Victoria was because he flattered her masterfully (and he readily admitted that he often laid it on pretty thick—"with a trowel"). More recently, Presidents Ronald Reagan and Bill Clinton both used an aptitude for paying compliments to help get elected and reelected. Had they not been so adept, American history might look very different. Even President Nixon paid attention to people's interests and activities and gave sincere, meaningful compliments—which helped to offset his famous awkwardness.

Fun fact: A 2008 study published in the journal *Neuron* found that giving someone a compliment activates the same reward center in the brain as paying him cash.

Politics isn't the only arena in which compliments come into play. Charles Schwab credited much of his business success to being "hearty in my approbation and lavish in my praise." Andrew Carnegie and John D. Rockefeller often used compliments to inspire employees and to help land big deals. Compliments can be effective at every level of a workplace hierarchy.

Even in the very warmest, friendliest, and simplest relations, flattery or praise is needed just as grease is needed to keep wheels going round.

—Leo Tolstoy

Compliments 101

HOW DO YOU PAY a proper compliment? If you absorb nothing else from this chapter, or any other part of this book, please take away this oh-so-crucial message: **Be sincere**. Mean it. Make the compliment honest and truthful. Do not fake or fabricate or falsify. You get the point.

We've all encountered individuals who, immediately upon seeing someone (anyone! everyone!), raise their voices an octave or two and gush something to the effect of, "Oh my *gawd*! You look soooooo awesome." Now, I'm guessing because you're reading this book that's not something you'd do, but come on. Does anyone who hears that think to herself, "Wow, I must really look soooooo awesome" and feel great for the rest of the day? Nope. Fake compliments are meaningless. Even if your version of false flattery isn't so extreme, don't bother. Others will probably be able to see right through it.

Okay, you're on board with sincerity. Now what?

Say it out loud

If a sincere compliment about someone pops into your head, why hold it back? We all do this, for a variety of reasons, including our own insecurities and the thought that the other person doesn't want or need to hear it. Get over that, and stop wasting opportunities to pay compliments. Don't skip it because you think the recipient already knows how you feel, or already knows how great she is. Believe me, she'd like to hear it again anyway. The author Washington Irving likely received a lot of praise but that didn't stop Charles Dickens from telling him, "What pleasure I have had in seeing and talking with you, I will not attempt to say. I shall never forget it as long as I live."

Put it in writing: A letter from Ludwig van Beethoven to his unnamed "Immortal Beloved"—which he never sent:

Good morning, on July 7

Though still in bed, my thoughts go out to you, my Immortal Beloved, now and then joyfully, then sadly, waiting to learn whether or not fate will hear us. I can live only wholly with you or not at all. Yes, I am resolved to wander so long away from you until I can fly to your arms and say that I am really at home with you, and can send my soul enwrapped in you into the land of spirits—Yes, unhappily it must be so. You will be the more contained since you know my fidelity to you. No one else can ever possess my heart, never—never. Oh God, why must one be parted from one whom one so loves. And yet my life in Vienna is now a wretched life—Your love makes me at once the happiest and the unhappiest of men. At my age I need a steady, quiet life—can that be so in our connection? My angel, I have just been told that the mailcoach goes every day—therefore I must close at once so that you may receive the letter at once. Be calm. Only by a calm consideration of our existence can we achieve our purpose to live together. Be calm—love me—today—yesterday.

What tearful longings for you— you—you—my life— my all—farewell. Oh continue to love me—never misjudge the most faithful heart of your beloved.

Ever thine.

Ever mine.

Ever ours.

We all love to receive compliments and
tend to appreciate those who offer them.
Therefore I often wonder why so few
people give them.

—*Emily Post's Etiquette*

Don't be indiscriminate with compliments

If you hear someone going around a party telling thirty guests they look gorgeous, will you believe it when she says the same thing to you? (We're not all supermodels, people.) When someone is known as a serial flatterer, his comments come to have little or no impact. As Samuel Johnson said, "He who praises everybody, praises nobody."

Fun fact: A 2003 study at the Kyoto Institute of Technology found that men and women are equally explicit in giving compliments, which contradicted earlier studies suggesting women are more explicit complimenters than men.

Keep it simple

Gushing and going over the top are signals of insincerity. If you do that, you're veering into fake flattery territory. There's just no need for that because the simple truth is plenty powerful. The key is not diluting the force of an honest compliment by being prone to exaggeration. If you say everything is amazing and beautiful and incredible, who's going to believe you when you apply one of those words to them? Say what you really think: "I like your haircut." "The dessert you made was delicious." "Your speech really struck a chord with me." That will be plenty.

> You're five foot nothin',
> a hundred and nothin', and you have
> barely a speck of athletic ability.
> And you hung in there with the best
> college football players in the
> land for two years.
> —Fortune to Rudy in *Rudy*

And remember that there's no need to go on and on and on. The more you say, in some cases, the less enjoyable a compliment becomes. "You look beautiful" works much better than, "Wow, you look really good in that dress. I mean, you look good in anything, but something about that dress really flatters you. Not that anything wouldn't flatter you. Um, where did you buy it?" Say what you mean, say it from the heart, and move on. Or, as Franklin D. Roosevelt said: "Be sincere; be brief; be seated."

George Washington reportedly relied on 110 rules from a book called *Rules of Civility and Decent Behavior in Company and Conversation.* Rule number 25, which effectually advised readers to keep compliments simple, is still a good one to follow: "Superfluous compliments and all affectation of ceremony are to be avoided, yet where due they are not to be neglected." (Number 12 is a good one too: "Bedew no man's face with your spittle by approaching too near him when you speak." Keep rule number 12 in mind when paying a compliment.)

Fun fact: The majority of compliments contain one of five adjectives (*nice, good, beautiful, pretty,* and *great*) or one of two verbs (*like* and *love*).

Avoid complimenting by comparison

Doing so could minimize your compliment. Telling an accomplished pastry chef, "This tart crust is as good as my grandmother's" diminishes her training. Or it might sound

insincere. Saying to a home baker, "This tart is better than anything Pierre Hermé could ever make," comes across as an exaggeration. (Pierre Hermé is a Parisian pastry chef considered by many to be the best in the world—which a home chef may or may not know, so the compliment doesn't work in that respect, either.) Just compliment the act or achievement itself, directly. Tell her you think the tart has a perfect crust and a deliciously sweet filling. Is anyone else in the mood for a tart right now?

Think before you speak

Phrase a compliment with a little care, so the recipient will know you thought about it and that what you're saying has real meaning. Be as specific as you can be. In other words—and I'll try to choose those other words carefully—even though it's wonderful to give a compliment right away when it's on your mind, take a moment to plan what you want to say and think about how best to express it, in a way that conveys your real meaning. Telling a friend, "That was fun!" after spending an afternoon engrossed in meaningful conversation with her isn't as accurate as saying something like, "I really loved our conversation today. Thanks for being a good listener. I'm lucky to have such an understanding friend."

Be not too hasty either with
praise or blame.

—Seneca

The American writer Kate Chopin said this about fellow writer Ruth McEnery Stuart: "Her voice in conversation has a melting quality that penetrates the senses, as some soothing ointment goes through the skin. Her eyes do not rest—they complete the charm begun by the voice, expression, and a thoroughly sympathetic manner. She is a delightful, womanly woman." It's clear Chopin thought about this and meant what she said. Saying "Ruth is great to talk to" just wouldn't have had the same effect.

Also, no matter what you're complimenting, quickly check the compliment before it flies out of your mouth to be sure you're not saying anything potentially patronizing or belittling.

But don't wait *too* long

If you only compliment grand achievements, you won't have many chances. Most of us don't do something splashy and newsworthy every single day, so look for something little to praise, like an impressive parallel parking job or an e-mail so witty it made you laugh out loud. As Emily Post wrote, "I urge you to speak up. The next time you have a nice thought about someone, tell him or her. If we all did it more frequently the world would be a happier place."

Make it personal

You don't always need to look for an act or accomplishment or physical trait to compliment—you can aim your desire to praise at a person and look for a quality of hers that's compliment-worthy. Have you admired her generosity, or the way kids seem to fall in love with her? Tell her that, whenever. When you consider a person you want to compliment, you're likely to come up with something that deserves a kind word.

Remember, a personal compliment doesn't have to be complicated. The writer Katherine Mansfield once told her friend, the painter Anne Estelle Rice, "I shall just go on rejoicing in the fact of you." That must have been nice to hear. And Rice didn't have to do anything in particular or achieve something grand in order to hear it.

Pay compliments in front of a crowd, at least sometimes

As much as we enjoy hearing people say nice things about us in private, it's a treat to get a shout-out in front of an audience. Hey, we're all a little vain. When others hear us being complimented, that usually makes us feel good, as long as the compliment isn't embarrassingly over-the-top, and we know we deserve it.

Admonish your friends privately, but praise them openly.

—Publilius Syrus

Say it with Facebook: Paying a public compliment is easier to do than ever. Just post it on Facebook or your preferred social networking site. Write a well-deserved compliment on a friend's wall so all 397 of her other friends can read it. Haven't seen her in a while? Tell her she looks gorgeous in her wedding photos or that her kids are adorable. Know what she's been up to? Congratulate her on her promotion, her book launch, or her store opening.

Remember that timing isn't everything, but it does matter

While there's no need to strategize and calculate the best exact second to issue a compliment—sincerity and spontaneity are far more important—at least be sure to compliment someone when she can hear it, and when she has time to appreciate it. Your admiration of your hostess's outfit amidst a sea of guests entering a party at the same time might not even register; if you tell her how hot she looks during a lull in the conversation or as you're leaving at the end of the night, the impact—and her pleasure—will be greater.

Also, try to pay a compliment as soon as possible after someone has done something to earn said compliment. If you've just watched your friend perform on stage, for example, tell him what you liked about the show right away when you see him backstage—that's when he is dying to hear something positive and his confidence may hinge in part on the reactions of others—instead of waiting for a week to share your verbal applause.

Compliment in such a way that the recipient feels comfortable

Be enthusiastic, not overly solicitous. Don't invade her personal space, use any intonation that makes the compliment sound like a come-on, or act too eager for a certain response. Present it simply, not scarily, and let it go.

Don't ruin it with any nonverbal attributes

An acquaintance recently approached me at a book signing to tell me how much he sincerely appreciated the new book. He's a gourmet type—it was a food and wine book—and he had specific things to say about why he liked it. But, apparently, he'd had a little too much food and wine and not enough floss and mouthwash in recent days, and he had some stinky breath. I didn't relish his praise. I just wanted to get away.

Unfortunate hygiene is even less fortunate if you're attempting to woo a potential love interest. You might have the sweetest, sincerest compliment ever—one that just might encourage her to keep talking to you—but if you let a loud and smelly one rip or you forgot the deodorant after a sweaty workout or she can still smell yesterday's egg salad on you . . . that conversation won't last long, and the compliment won't be what she remembers.

So when you're telling someone how beautiful her eyes are, don't get all up in her face with garlic breath. And if you want to exclaim how impressed you are by a plate of homemade truffles, say it, don't spray it—not at the truffle-maker and definitely not on the truffles.

The most potent compliment will fizzle if uttered with stench or visible spittle.

—Willis Goth Regier

Expect nothing in return

When you issue a compliment, have no anticipation of *anything* coming back to you. Don't compliment someone because you want him to do you a favor. (That's one of the signs of an insincere compliment; read more on page 119.) Don't give a compliment because you're fishing for a compliment in return, either. Telling your friend she looks gorgeous does not obligate her to ooh and aah over how fabulous *you* are; in fact, if she did so, that would only minimize your compliment to her.

The only thing you should want to take away from paying a compliment is the happy sensation that accompanies saying or doing a kind thing. "If we are so contemptibly selfish that we can't radiate a little happiness and pass on a bit of appreciation without trying to get something out of the other person in return," Dale Carnegie wrote, "if our souls are no bigger than sour crab apples, we shall meet with the failure we so richly deserve."

6 Selfish Reasons to Pay a Compliment

First, a caveat: As I already mentioned, you should never have an ulterior motive for giving a compliment. If you do, the compliment won't be sincere, and it will fall flat. But if you need a little extra incentive to adopt the complimenting habit, it just so happens that offering up sincere compliments (when you expect nothing in return) has some nice side effects for the giver.

> A beauty is a woman you notice; a charmer is one who notices you.
>
> —Adlai Stevenson

1. Making someone else feel good makes you feel great too. There is even scientific evidence to back this up. It's probably part of what motivates us to volunteer our time for causes we care about and donate money to charity.

2. People will like being around you. If you're a lovely person who pays thoughtful, wonderful compliments,

folks are going to gravitate toward you. Assuming you're a people person, this is a good thing.

3. Paying compliments speaks volumes about your character. Someone who gives praise freely instead of spreading rumors is much nicer than a gossip girl.

4. It makes you look altruistic. Focusing on someone else's good qualities means you're not utterly self-absorbed.

5. Some studies suggest that people who give compliments are perceived as smarter than those who don't.

6. You may be inspired. Noticing that someone else has done something well or achieved something impressive, and deepening that impression by commenting on it, you just might give yourself a kick in the ass to get working on your own good deeds.

Virtues are acquired through endeavor, which rests wholly upon yourself. So to praise others for their virtues can but encourage one's own efforts.

—Thomas Paine

The Secret to Great Compliments: Listen Up!

IF YOU WANT TO deliver a compliment that will really mean something to the recipient, start by simply paying attention to what she says and does, and then thinking about what matters to her.

Has a friend been working hard to get back into shape, with good results? Don't just comment on her weight; tell her how fit she is. Did an obsessive foodie invite you over for the best supper you've had in months? Compliment the execution of the most delicious dish, not the platter it was served on. But then for the stylish gal who served you takeout and cares way more about decor than, say, perfecting her demi-glace, please, compliment her impeccable taste in tableware.

The most seductive flattery flatters the You you wish to be.

—Willis Goth Regier

With people you know even a little, it's not hard to figure out how to strike a chord. As Philip Stanhope (a.k.a. Lord Chesterfield) wrote in a letter to his son, "Sincere praise is always good. You will easily discover every man's prevailing vanity by observing his favorite topic of conversation, for every man talks most of what he has most a mind to be thought to excel in. Touch him there and you touch him to the quick." It's good advice, and it has been for a long time: Chesterfield's *Letters to His Son* first came out in 1774, and many versions of it are still in print.

And how, exactly, do you learn what matters most to your friends and loved ones? It's not difficult. **Listen.** Good listeners can easily become good complimenters (not to mention good conversationalists, good colleagues, and good confidants, but let's stay on point here). Though former White House Social Secretary Letitia Baldridge has said that listening has become a lost art—and, sadly, she's right—it's a skill that's not hard to learn. And while listening can certainly give you great material for compliments, remember that the act of listening itself is a pretty nice compliment too. When you listen carefully to someone, you make him feel important. As Mary Kay, head of the direct sales cosmetics empire, pointed out, "Everyone has an invisible sign hanging from her neck saying, 'Make me feel important.'"

Exclusive attention to the person who is speaking to you is very important. Nothing else is so flattering as that.

—Celebrated listener Charles William Eliot, the longest serving president of Harvard University

Here are a few tips for listening well:

Do. Not. Interrupt

Let the person who's talking finish what she has to say, please.

When you're having a conversation with someone, look her in the eye

This isn't a staring contest—you're allowed to blink—but focus on the person who's speaking and don't let your eyes dart around the room. If your eyes on are everything but her, she might think you're trying to get away or looking for someone better to talk to, and then she's not going to want to share anything.

Ask questions

This is the easiest conversational trick around—if you keep asking questions (questions related to the conversation, that is), you will never be at a loss for something to say, and the person you're speaking to will be encouraged to share more, especially if you ask questions about topics that interest her. Has she recently traveled? Press for details about her favorite sites. Did she mention taking a photography class? Find out what she likes to shoot.

Visions of greatness: Keep in mind as you're listening closely that people love to get compliments on those traits and skills they aspire to, not just the ones they already know they have. It might sound like a cliché, but the woman who has been told she's beautiful all her life loves hearing about how smart she is. A friend of mine who studied incessantly and didn't have much of a social life in high school or college now basks in compliments about what a good friend she is.

Remember what you talked about

No, there won't be a quiz later. But don't drift off and start thinking about work, the weather, or your next cocktail. Focus on what she's saying, and take away a key point or two to remember—it could be the subject of a killer compliment sometime soon.

Jackie O. was a master at attentive listening, and her skill in that arena—making people feel like they were the center of her universe—is often cited as a reason why she was so beloved.

Barbara Walters, who has made a career out of listening to people, wrote admiringly in her memoir, *Audition,* about observing the listening skills of her fellow journalist and celebrated Washington hostess Joan Braden: "She was all eyes and had the ability to look fascinated at will—so there'd she be looking up in awe while the guy was looking down at his obviously devoted subject. Then, too, she laughed at every joke someone told, and rarely talked about herself. Almost everything she said seemed to come out as a question that would produce an answer. And every conversation, whether with a man or a woman, included a compliment."

Complimentary Topics

HOPEFULLY, ONCE YOU know *how* to give a compliment, you won't be at a loss for specific compliment ideas. You don't need to have a slate of them ready to go; spontaneous compliments should be inspired by something you notice in the moment. But in case you're still wondering where to look for inspiration, here are a few things upon which most people enjoy being complimented.

Smarts

If a friend does something clever, compliment it. We all want to think we're smart cookies, and a compliment to someone's intelligence is always welcomed. I asked friends about their favorite compliments, and many of them mentioned praise that made them feel brainy and competent. My friend Mindy, who advises clients on issues of wealth management that I won't pretend to understand fully, told me the best compliment she received was in the wake of a recent round of economic turmoil (make that economic panic): "A longtime client called while the market was crashing around me and told me that I put his mind at ease and make him comfortable no matter what's happening," she recalled. "That made me feel capable and good at my job, and his saying it probably kept me from drinking an entire bottle of gin that night."

> You're braver than you believe, and stronger than you seem, and smarter than you think.
>
> —Christopher Robin to Winnie the Pooh

Wit

Just as it's nice to feel smart, many of us like to think we're funny. The nicest compliment I got about a book

I wrote last year came from a friend who told me she laughed out loud while she read parts of it. (Luckily, she was referring to the parts that were supposed to be funny.) Laugh freely and openly when someone says something humorous, and let her know she cracks you up. Laughter is so good for us (according to the Mayo Clinic, it reduces stress, improves our immune function, relieves pain, and soothes stomachaches)—shouldn't we thank those who give us the giggles with a compliment? I am eternally grateful to those friends of mine who keep me doubled over in laughter, and I think I owe it to them to let them know that.

Looks

Call me shallow, but I'm more confident when I think I'm looking good than when I feel like a frump. If you are entirely unfazed by thoughts of appearance, *mazel tov*. (Oh yeah, and you're a liar.) It may lack substance but a sincere compliment about someone's appearance is always a hit. Be careful here, though, and don't make this your automatic go-to compliment. It's a fairly easy one to give even when you don't *really* mean it, and that—of course—makes it worthless. I have a friend who compliments my outfit every single time I see her. I'd like to think I'm that well-dressed, but I'm not. When she complimented my attire one morning after I'd been up till two in the morning on deadline and rolled out to get a latte wearing sweats and a baseball cap, the jig was completely up.

I was informed that you were the most beautiful woman ever to visit Casablanca. That was a gross understatement.

—Captain Renault to Ilsa in *Casablanca*

Fun fact: In a study at Willamette University, men gave women twice as many compliments about appearance as women gave men.

Try to be more specific when complimenting someone's appearance than, "You look cute." If someone does happen to look indescribably cute, that's fine, but even better is to tell her that her skin is glowing or that her hair looks radiant and shiny or that her body looks hot in her jeans and tee.

Every now and then the all-encompassing looks compliment is appropriate, but be sure to deliver it with a lot of enthusiasm when someone is truly looking fabulous. On our wedding day, when my almost-husband saw me for the first time, he gaped a little bit and told me, "You look amazing." I didn't need him to call out tiny details about my dress or hair. What he said was plenty, and I'll never forget how good it felt to hear him say it.

Taste

People love hearing that they have great taste, so this is a wonderful attribute to compliment. It feels fantastic when someone admires your discernment and judgment. You feel smart, savvy, and stylish all at once. Thanking her friend Ethel Sands for a gift, Virginia Woolf once said, "How can you divine my tastes so exactly—what's more, add to them your own exquisitry?" That compliment acknowledged Sands's thoughtfulness as well as her taste—a double whammy.

Some of my favorite taste compliments to receive are the ones about my home. When my friend Meg visited me from New York and told me my little apartment in the Back Bay in Boston felt like home, I felt warm and fuzzy inside. And I'll admit that, when someone walks into the apartment I share with my husband in San Francisco—where he lived for eight years before I got there, formerly with roommates whose ideas of decorating included halogen lamps, circa-1981 plastic coffee tables, and a TV perched on a milk carton—and exclaims how good it looks now, I feel proud. Granted, just about anything I did would have been a huge improvement. Still, I like when someone appreciates my effort. If you think your friends have great taste in furniture or literature or houses or spouses, let them know.

Fun fact: Both men and women are more likely to give a compliment to a member of the same sex than to a member of the opposite sex.

Skills

"Girls only want boyfriends who have great skills," Napoleon Dynamite told Pedro in his eponymous movie. Napoleon was referring, obviously, to nunchuck skills, bow-hunting skills, and computer hacking skills. (If you haven't seen the movie, put it in your Netflix queue. It will make you laugh and that's very good for you. See page 28 if you want to know why.) In terms of compliments, I'd revise that bit of wisdom to, "Girls want boyfriends who compliment their skills." And people like friends and family members who praise their skills too. Compliment the chef on his cooking skills, the knitter on her sweater-making skills, the carpenter on her bench-building skills. If she's passionate about something—and you notice she's done it well—I guarantee she'd love to hear it.

The pianist Clara Schumann told the composer Johannes Brahms, "You have literally bewitched me with some of the melodies in your new pieces. I have not been able to get them out of my head for days." Especially coming from another musician, that was probably a bewitching compliment for Brahms to hear, addressing as it did his skills and passions.

Uniqueness

Most people love to be reminded of how special they are. My friend Stacey, a business school graduate who has followed a successful straight-and-narrow career path, said the nicest compliment she ever received was from a classmate who called her "quirky." She explained that it made her feel "funny, interesting, and different—like I wasn't your run-of-the-mill B-school type." But be careful here, and avoid anything that might be construed as a backhanded compliment. (Complimenting an accent, for example, could be taken as criticism.)

Friendship

Among the people I polled, compliments about being a good friend were the hands-down favorite. Simply saying, "You're a good friend" compliments a variety of qualities all at once; telling someone *why* she is such a good friend will also resonate. "The nicest compliment I've received is that I'm a thoughtful and loyal person," my friend Aimee told me. (And she's someone who gets complimented all the time on her taste, style, looks, and smarts.) If someone is a wonderful friend, be a good friend back and share that with her.

9 Occasions When You Should Really, Really Try to Pay a Compliment

1. Your best friend has just been dumped or cheated on

This is not the time to criticize her taste in significant others. If there's even a hint of an I-told-you-so fluttering about your consciousness, keep it to yourself. Nor is it the time—and this *should* go without saying—to explain what she does wrong in relationships. Her ego has likely taken a beating, so give it the salve it needs with a sincere compliment. Keep it sassy and decidedly nonpatronizing—tell her what a hot, sexy catch she is, and then take her out for a cocktail and let her know how often she's getting checked out.

2. Meeting your future in-laws (or people you hope will become your in-laws)

No, you don't need to suck up to them or pretend to be anything you're not. Grand,

dramatic, or overly personal compliments don't belong in this scenario. But hey, you like their offspring quite a bit—why not tell them that? Your significant other wouldn't be here without them. A simple "I've never met anyone as thoughtful as your son" or "Your daughter is so talented" should make them feel a little happy and proud.

3. Your fiancé was recently laid off

This is a time to be especially subtle, because too much unsolicited praise could be interpreted as pity. And that doesn't do much good for a deflated ego. Request help with a project, rave about one of his best moves in the bedroom, and slip in a low-key compliment about his qualifications or skills when he's applying for a new job.

4. You just watched your sister perform in front of a live audience

Whether she's on Broadway or in a school auditorium, giving a speech to thousands or reading her poetry at open-mike night, when she steps off that stage and says hello to you, she

craves your approval and positive feedback. So don't be stingy about it. Find *something* worth complimenting, even if you weren't wowed by the whole show. Praise her stage presence, her beautiful look, her sultry voice, or a specific turn of phrase. If you can remember something she said or sang exactly, even better—that shows you were paying attention, which is another subtle compliment. (Two good compliments mean major sisterly brownie points, not that you were after those.)

5. You're greeting the bride at her wedding

Be *sure* to compliment the bride on her big day. You might have moaned and groaned about having to shell out cash for a plane ticket, hotel room, and new dress—but get over yourself. She's a friend or relative of yours, and whether it's a backyard barbecue or a blowout ballroom bonanza for five hundred, the bride has been blissfully anticipating this occasion for months. Or years. Or more. This is her moment, and it doesn't matter how many people have told her how gorgeous she looks and how wonderful everything is. She wants to hear it again, and again, and again. Since she's probably glowing, finding something to compliment shouldn't be much of a stretch. So don't forget to pay a compliment in your rush to get your first glass of champagne, please. Even if the wedding isn't done in your taste (you hate the pouffy brides-maid dresses and the enormous ice sculptures), you can find something to comment on kindly and honestly. Maybe her hair looks beautiful? Or her dress is perfect for her? Or her flowers are breathtaking? Or maybe none of that matters because she just looks so in love. If that's the case, tell her. She'll be thrilled to hear it.

6. You're visiting with a pregnant woman

Even a woman who claims to enjoy every minute of waddling around with a creature growing inside of her has phases when she feels less than attractive, less than coordinated, and less than sexy. She doesn't need you to gape at her and tell her she's huge or ask if she's carrying triplets. (So what if she is carrying triplets? That's still an unfortunate question.) Find something—any-thing—to compliment: her shiny hair, perhaps, or her radiant skin or (if you're a close female friend) her suddenly X-rated ta-tas. (Seriously— a woman who gets boobs when she's pregnant

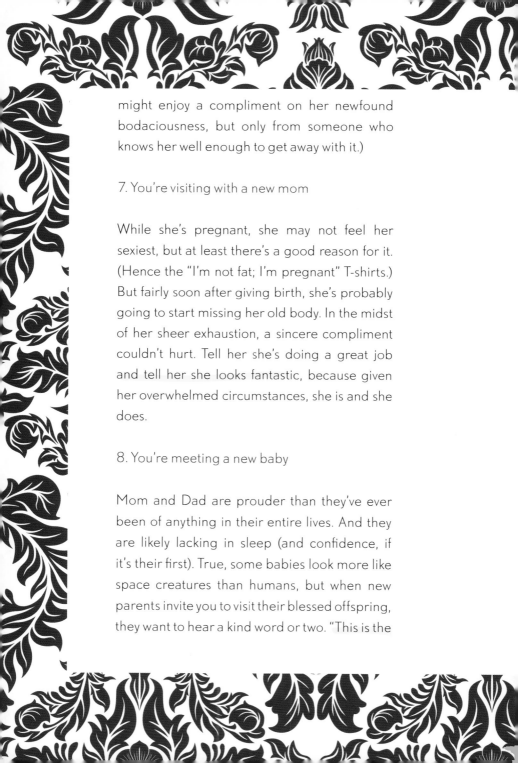

might enjoy a compliment on her newfound bodaciousness, but only from someone who knows her well enough to get away with it.)

7. You're visiting with a new mom

While she's pregnant, she may not feel her sexiest, but at least there's a good reason for it. (Hence the "I'm not fat; I'm pregnant" T-shirts.) But fairly soon after giving birth, she's probably going to start missing her old body. In the midst of her sheer exhaustion, a sincere compliment couldn't hurt. Tell her she's doing a great job and tell her she looks fantastic, because given her overwhelmed circumstances, she is and she does.

8. You're meeting a new baby

Mom and Dad are prouder than they've ever been of anything in their entire lives. And they are likely lacking in sleep (and confidence, if it's their first). True, some babies look more like space creatures than humans, but when new parents invite you to visit their blessed offspring, they want to hear a kind word or two. "This is the

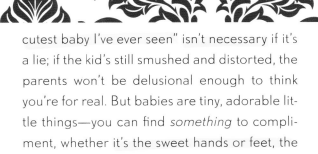

cutest baby I've ever seen" isn't necessary if it's a lie; if the kid's still smushed and distorted, the parents won't be delusional enough to think you're for real. But babies are tiny, adorable little things—you can find *something* to compliment, whether it's the sweet hands or feet, the perky nose, or the preciously plump little legs.

9. Someone is having a really bad day

Maybe she was dumped, laid off, *and* splashed by a cab speeding through a mud puddle within a twenty-four-hour time frame. Or maybe she's just feeling blue and can't pinpoint why. Propping her up with a compliment might not fix everything today, but it could help tomorrow look a little rosier. Tell your coworker she's been doing a great job; tell your friend how beautiful she is; tell your mom you love her and appreciate all she's done for you. Having you notice something about them and take the time to say something lets people know you're thinking about them. And that is a delightful compliment in and of itself.

Foreign affairs: First, a tip: Be careful about complimenting someone's foreign accent. A compliment on someone's accent—telling her "your accent is so interesting" or "it's so beautiful"—could be construed as patronizing or critical. Unless you know someone very well, it's best to avoid that. It's fine to ask where someone is from but don't focus on the accent.

Also be aware that compliments are given and received differently in other cultures. In the Netherlands, for example, compliments tend to be very low-key (and that might be an overstatement) and infrequently given. And for Chinese people, accepting compliments isn't really acceptable. "In Chinese culture, compliments are discouraged and humility is encouraged," my friend Joanne, who is Chinese, explained. "You are taught to deflect compliments—see *The Joy Luck Club*—and never ever to admit that you agree with the compliment given."

Compliments in Love
(and Lust)

WHEN YOU ARE in love with some-
one—or even just in like with someone you're
starting to date—there is no good reason not
to compliment this person generously and
often. You dig him. You've chosen him out of
all the other fish in the sea. Let him know
that, and tell him why. Early in a relationship, compliments add fuel to the flirtation
fire. Once a relationship is established (and

after it's been going on for years), compliments remind your better half that you still appreciate him, still dig him, still know he's the fish you want.

Love delights in praises.

—William Shakespeare

Let's face it: A good compliment can be a serious turn-on, whether you've been with someone for three dates or three years. If you want to get some, try opening up with a sincere compliment or two. I'm much more likely to want to hook up with someone—only my husband, these days, but this has always been true—if he lets me know that he thinks I'm awesome (and hot) than if he forgets to mention it.

"Compliment your partner daily," wrote Les and Leslie Parrot, authors of *Saving Your Marriage Before It Starts.* "The most important element of romantic passion for both husbands and wives is to feel special. Not only do they want to feel sexually attractive to their mates, but they want to know they are appreciated. Compliments feel good—both to give and to receive."

This is vital in the early stages of a relationship as well as years into it, in good times and difficult. Isabel Burton told her husband, Richard, a nineteenth-century explorer and travel writer, "I would rather have a crust and a tent with you than be queen of all the world."

No matter how busy you are, there's always time for a compliment. Whether or not you agree with their politics, you can take a lesson on this from some of the men

---

Put it in writing: Excerpt of a letter from Dwight Eisenhower to Mamie Eisenhower:

My sweet heart—

By the time you read this your newspapers will probably have told you where I am and you will understand why your birthday letter had to be written some time in advance . . .

Anyway—on the day you open this letter you'll be 46. I'd like to be there to help you celebrate, and to kiss you 46 times (multiplied by any number you care to pick) . . . In any event I will be with you in thought, and entirely aside from the usual congratulations and felicitations I will be thinking with the deepest gratitude of the many happy hours and years you've given me . . .

The crowning thing you've given me is our son—he has been so wonderful, unquestionably because he's so much you—that I find I live in him so very often. Your love and our son have been my greatest gifts from life, and on your birthday I wish that my powers of expression were such as to make you understand that thoroughly—clearly and for always. I've never wanted any other wife—you're mine, and for that reason I've been luckier than any other man. . . *too bad he wasn't sincere!*

43

who have served as president of the United States. George Bush wrote to Barbara Pierce, soon after their engagement, "How lucky our children will be to have a mother like you." He also wrote "Goodnite, my beautiful. Everytime I say beautiful you about kill me, but you'll have to accept it." (Apparently, future first ladies have trouble accepting compliments too.) After almost three decades of marriage, Ronald Reagan wrote to Nancy Reagan, "You have made one man (me) the most happy man in the world for 29 years." They were together happily for twenty-three more.

> ## Marge, you're as pretty as Princess Leia and as smart as Yoda.
> —Homer Simpson

Barack Obama complimented Michelle Obama publicly and earnestly when he wrote, at the end of his memoir *Dreams from My Father*:

"I think I've learned to be more patient these past few years, with others as well as myself. If so, it's one of several improvements in my character that I attribute to my wife, Michelle. She's a daughter of the South Side, raised in one of those bungalow-style houses that I spent so many hours visiting during my first year in Chicago. She doesn't always know what to make of me; she worries that, like Gramps and the Old Man, I am something of a dreamer. Indeed, in her eminent practicality, she reminds me not a little of [Obama's beloved grandmother] Toot. I remember how, the first time I took her back to Hawaii, Gramps nudged my ribs and said Michelle was quite 'a looker.' Toot, on

Put it in writing: A letter from Mark Twain (Samuel L. Clemens) to his wife, Livy, on her thirtieth birthday:

Livy darling,

Six years have gone by since I made my first great success in life and won you, and thirty years have passed since Providence made preparation for that happy success by sending you into the world. Every day we live together adds to the security of my confidence, that we can never any more wish to be separated than that we can ever imagine a regret that we were joined. You are dearer to me to-day, my child, than you were upon the last anniversary of this birth-day; you were dearer then than you were a year before—you have grown more and more dear from the first of those anniversaries, and I do not doubt that this precious progression will continue on to the end.

Let us look forward to the coming anniversaries, with their age and their gray hairs without fear and without depression, trusting and believing that the love we bear each other will be sufficient to make them blessed.

So, with abounding affection for you and our babies, I hail this day that brings you the matronly grace and dignity of three decades!

Always yours,

S.L.C.

the other hand, described my bride-to-be as 'a very sensible girl'—which Michelle understood to be my grandmother's highest form of praise."

It is very difficult for a man to even speak to someone who looks like you.

—Hitch to Sara in *Hitch*

Compliments aren't just for those already in a relationship. When you're crushing on someone, a good sincere compliment can't hurt your cause. No, it might not turn unrequited love into a passionate affair. (Though you never know; one of the most celebrated romances of all time began when Robert Browning sent Elizabeth Barrett a complimentary letter that began, "I love your verses with all my heart." No flimsy flattery there.) But it could help someone see you through a more romantic lens or tip him off that your interest might be a little more than platonic. My friend Marc told me that sincere compliments from a woman interested in him "are 100 percent effective with me." And they're necessary to let him know what the woman is thinking, too, because, "I don't pick up on many of the other cues on that stuff," he said.

If you pay attention to some of the best romantic lines in movies, you may notice they are often sincere and creative compliments. Sure, these all come from scriptwriters, but they are good—and a good reminder that romantic compliments can be a little mushy and still be wonderful.

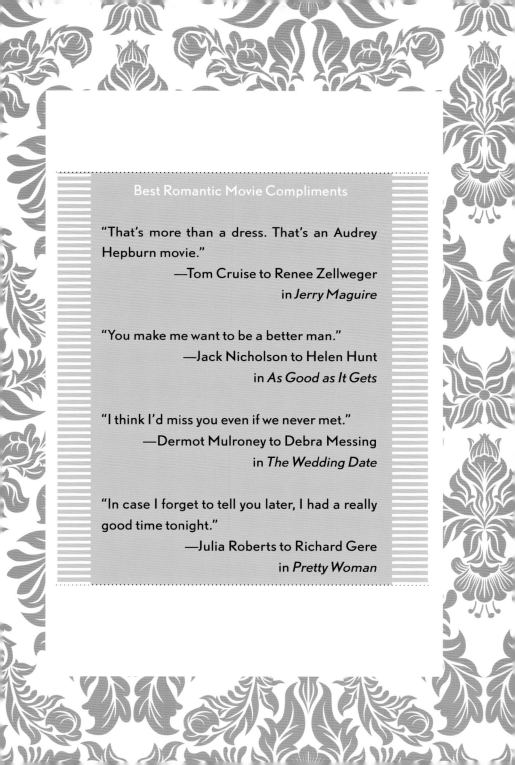

Best Romantic Movie Compliments

"That's more than a dress. That's an Audrey Hepburn movie."

—Tom Cruise to Renee Zellweger
in *Jerry Maguire*

"You make me want to be a better man."

—Jack Nicholson to Helen Hunt
in *As Good as It Gets*

"I think I'd miss you even if we never met."

—Dermot Mulroney to Debra Messing
in *The Wedding Date*

"In case I forget to tell you later, I had a really good time tonight."

—Julia Roberts to Richard Gere
in *Pretty Woman*

There are good lines on TV, too. One night, when I probably should have been writing, I watched a rerun of *Friends*. It was the one when you learn how Chandler and Monica really got together. Turns out, the relationship started with a compliment—he told her, sincerely, "You were the most beautiful woman in the room. You're the most beautiful woman in any room." Okay, I know it's an out-of-date television sitcom but without a great line like that, there's no way it makes sense for Monica to hop in bed with Chandler.

This can work like a charm in real life. "A guy in college told me that when he saw me, he got butterflies," said my friend Aimee, who had not known she was the object of this guy's crush. "I was flattered and found it so sweet that I ended up dating him . . . for years!"

My friend Margo admitted that she has "been a sucker in the past for attractive guys who throw me compliments, but it has to be something witty and not contrived or cliché." And my brother, Seth, recalled, "Someone with a crush on me complimented my play in a soccer game that I didn't even know she was watching. It wasn't just the fact that she was at the game but the detail with which she remembered the play that made me think twice about her."

If I know what love is,
it is because of you.

—Herman Hesse

When paying a compliment to someone you don't really know—but would like to know better, romantically—remember that there's a difference between a sincere compliment and a pickup line. First and foremost, consider what you hope to get from it. If you say something flattering but you have an ulterior motive (say, you're angling for a little one-night nooky), that's going to come across. You might score the hook-up but that's not a good compliment. You've got to go into it expecting nothing in return. What's more, you need to say something you *mean*. Don't make up a line just so you have something to say. It will sound cheesy, guaranteed. Notice something that really deserves a compliment and tell the object of your interest the truth about it. Finally, don't be creepy with an innuendo-laden comment. You don't know this person—why frighten him? Be nice, be sincere, and be tasteful. Then just wait and see what kind of effect it has. If nothing else, you'll make someone feel pretty good for a few minutes.

An article in *Cosmopolitan*, that sage source of information on all things sexy, offered this bit of truly sound advice on compliments for your love interest: "The more specific you get when you praise a woman, the more she'll eat it up." Instead of just saying, "You look nice," the article suggested, "You look awesome in that dress" or, even more specifically, "Your eyes look awesome when you wear that color." That last one takes a little extra thought, of course, which (as you probably realize by now) is one of the keys to giving a great compliment. Cite precise aspects of your significant other's outfit or body or face. But please, steer clear of specific references to a woman's weight. Even if you tell her, "That skirt makes you look skinny," she *may* start to wonder if other skirts make her look fat. Trust me—don't go there.

Focus on more than appearances. Compliment a specific talent ("Your serve is impossible to return" or—brace yourself, gentlemen—"You're a really good driver"); a lovable personality trait; phenomenal skills in bed (if you liked a particular maneuver, and want to experience it again, compliment it!); and the specific, special way your significant other makes you feel. One day it occurred to me that the sound of my husband's voice is my favorite sound on the planet and hearing it, even when he's speaking to someone else, gives me a little thrill. So I told him that. He liked hearing it. Easy.

Guys are less likely than gals to get excited about a compliment to their eyes or their outfit, so when giving a romantic compliment to the male of the species, focus on strength (I've been known to compliment perfectly defined calf muscles); sense of humor (laugh unabashedly when he cracks a funny—if it is, in fact, funny); achievements; and general sexiness (a man wants to know if you want him). If he's the father of your child, don't be afraid to let him know what a great parent he is. My friend Carrie said her husband loves when she tells him what a good job he does providing for their family and how much they all appreciate him.

Don't worry that compliments will make your partner egotistical or cause him to stop doing the things you love because he doesn't think he needs to anymore. That won't happen. If anything, he'll be more eager to please. As *Peter Pan* playwright J. M. Barrie noted, "The praise that comes from love does not make us vain, but more humble."

And if you ever find yourself caught in a moment when you really want to pay a compliment to someone you love—but are so lovestruck you can't think of anything to say—try "I love you." Expressed honestly and from the heart, it's one of the nicest compliments there is.

You've got to have friends: Lovers aren't the only ones who want and need compliments. Your friends—who've stood by you through crushes, breakups, and heartbreaks—should get them too. So remember to heap a little praise on pals in the midst of all the compliments to your significant other(s).

Tell a friend how proud you are of her, how much she makes you laugh, and that you always have fun with her. Notice when she accomplishes something, puts together a really great outfit, or does something thoughtful for you—and tell her that you notice. Say it in person, on the phone, via e-mail, in a text, or in a handwritten note. Do it when she's having a bad day, and when she's having a good day, too.

And remember that just about anytime, in any format, she'd be thrilled to hear this from you: "I'm lucky to have you as a friend."

6 Compliments Guys Love to Get (from a Lover)

1. You're the hottest guy I know.

2. I want you.

3. Your body really turns me on.

4. You have incredible, strong arms. (Or another specific compliment to a manly part of the body that turns you on.)

5. Oh my. (In an awestruck tone of voice, in response to seeing a certain part of his anatomy for the first time.)

6. That was amazing. (Referring to a specific act or an entire session—guys and gals both enjoy having their confidence boosted in the bedroom.)

6 Compliments Gals Love to Get (from a Lover)

1. You're the most beautiful woman I know.

2. I miss you.

3. Your body really turns me on.

4. You have incredible, sexy legs. (Or another compliment to a specific feminine part of the body that turns you on.)

5. I love falling asleep with you. (Or cuddling with you, or hugging you.)

6. That was amazing. (Whether you're referring to a specific act or an entire session, this builds confidence and is great to hear.)

Put it in writing: Sonnet 18:

Shall I compare thee to a summer's day?
Thou art more lovely and more temperate:
Rough winds do shake the darling buds of May,
And summer's lease hath all too short a date;
Sometime too hot the eye of heaven shines,
And often is his gold complexion dimm'd;
And every fair from fair sometime declines,
By chance or nature's changing course untrimm'd;
But thy eternal summer shall not fade,
Nor lose possession of that fair thou ow'st;
Nor shall Death brag thou wander'st in his shade,
When in eternal lines to time thou growest:
So long as men can breathe or eyes can see,
So long lives this, and this gives life to thee.
- William Shakespeare

Working the Compliment

A COMPLIMENT FROM a coworker or boss, or even a friend who knows something about your professional prowess, can be inspiring. Contrary to what some managers seem to think, it does *not* encourage laziness. No one gets a work-related compliment and thinks, "Sweet, I can slack off now." The opposite is true: A compliment is a powerful motivator.

Compliments may stir the recipient to continue and even intensify her endeavors. When you pay a compliment to someone on her impressive effort or excellent results, you encourage her to keep up the good work—and maybe even work a little harder. You help perpetuate whatever positive thing she's doing.

The desire to be worthy of the praise we receive strengthens our powers of virtue; and the praise bestowed on our wit, our courage, and our appearance helps to enhance them.

—François de La Rochefoucauld

Far and wide, employees rank appreciation and recognition at the top of their lists of motivational factors in the workplace. So it is not surprising that statistics from the U.S. Department of Labor suggest feeling unappreciated is a leading cause of leaving a job. "Abilities wither under criticism; they blossom under encouragement. To become a more effective leader of people," Dale Carnegie wrote, "praise the slightest improvement and praise every improvement."

Especially if someone is struggling, a compliment can do wonders. "The smallest gesture, kind comment, genuine word of encouragement, quick compliment, or praise for a job well done can make a lasting difference in someone's life," wrote Glenn Van Ekeren in *12 Simple Secrets of Happiness at Work*.

While colleagues are the most obvious targets for work-related encouragement, friends might appreciate it, too. "I was experiencing a bit of the frustration that comes with the territory of trying to make it on your own—that is, trying to survive without a corporate job," my brother's roommate Jesse told me, "when a friend of mine who makes a significant salary from a large firm said to me that he would give anything to be able to leave the chains of corporate life behind and that he was jealous of my ability to do so. He said that despite the hardship of walking my own path, he and others admired me for taking that risk." That was all Jesse needed to hear. He was inspired to stay on the entrepreneurial path, and he's still on it.

When you do need to offer constructive criticism at work, try to open with a sincere compliment. This reminds the person you're criticizing that they are doing plenty that's positive, which may inspire them to work harder instead of retreating into self-pity. When Benjamin Franklin was a teenager, his father read some of his letters and found them lacking in "elegance of expression, in method, and in perspicuity." But because dear old dad first explained what was *good* about his writing, young Ben was inspired to get even better rather than give up, and he embarked on a rigorous, self-initiated course of writing practice. Obviously, that worked out pretty well; Franklin was dubbed America's "first great man of letters" by the Scottish philosopher David Hume.

Put it in writing: Excerpt of a letter from Charles Dickens to Mary Ann Evans (also known as George Eliot):

Dear Sir:

I have been so strongly affected by the first two tales in the book you have had the kindness to send to me through Messrs. Blackwood, that I hope you will excuse my writing to you to express my admiration of their extraordinary merit. The exquisite truth and delicacy, both of the humor and the pathos of the stories, I have never seen the like of; and they have impressed me in a manner that I should find it very difficult to describe to you, if I had the impertinence to try.

In addressing these few words of thankfulness to the creator of the sad fortunes of Mr. Amos Barton, and the sad love-story of Mr. Gilfil, I am (I presume) bound to adopt the name that it pleases that excellent writer to assume. I can suggest no better one; but I should have been strongly disposed, if I had been left to my own devices, to address the said writer as a woman. I have observed what seems to me to be such womanly touches, in those moving fictions, that the assurance on the title-page is insufficient to satisfy me, even now. If they originated with no woman, I believe that no man ever before had the art of making himself, mentally, so like a woman, since the world began.

Michael: Attention please. Jan Levinson's coming very soon and so we're going to have our weekly suggestion box meeting. So you can get in your constructive compliments ASAP.
Ryan: Don't you mean "constructive criticism"?
Michael: What did I say?
Kelly: You said "constructive compliments." That doesn't make any sense.
Michael: Well Kelly, that was neither constructive nor a compliment, so maybe you should stop criticizing my English and start making some suggestions. 'Kay?
—The Office

"I believe in giving a person incentive to work," Charles Schwab once said. "So I am anxious to praise but loath to find fault." Bosses should praise deserving employees, and colleague-to-colleague compliments can be incredibly inspiring, as can a compliment from a worker to her manager.

When my friend Joanne, who owns a bakery, heard that a pastry chef who used to work for her said she was a fair, kind, generous employer who treats her employees well, she said, "It hit me like a ton of bricks, in a nice way, because it's always been my goal to be good to people and do the right thing." Joanne went on: "I have worked hard to be that kind of boss, and to hear that my employees actually notice and appreciate it really meant a lot to me. It's one of the nicest compliments I've ever received." When you do compliment your boss, though, just be mindful of who's listening. This is one case in which you may want to pay the compliment in private, so no one interprets it as sucking up.

"Appreciation in the workplace is the most underutilized and valuable currency," explained Debbie Goldstein, a managing director at Triad Consulting, a firm specializing in communication and conflict resolution. "We are free with criticism, but not with appreciation. But research has shown that people need to feel appreciation from the people who work with them. That can come in the form of a compliment."

The key, Goldstein said, is that you shouldn't give any form of compliment if it's not authentic. In a work environment, just as in a personal environment, the ramifications of a fake compliment are serious. "If your internal voice says a person is doing a horrible job, and what you say out loud to them is, 'great job' the gap will be apparent. As hard as we try to stifle content in our head, it leaks out. Our tone of voice and body language reveal that we're being insincere. And if what you think and what you say are not aligned, people sense that." In terms of building trust and strengthening relationships, Goldstein said that's one of the worst things you can do. So again—with any and every compliment you give—sincerity is the most important quality.

At work, you should also watch *what* you compliment. While with friends it's generally fine to praise whatever pops into your head, at the office, Goldstein said, "Don't be too personal. Don't cross that line. If there's a chance it could be misconstrued as unprofessional, especially if you don't know the person well, be careful." Avoid compliments about appearance or—obviously—anything even remotely sexual and focus on praising working style as well as products and results.

Straightforward work-related compliments are welcomed and appreciated, but compliments that stray from the professional sphere *could* lead to discomfort, misinterpretation, and other problems. My friend Mandy told me, "A client came up to me not long ago and told me I really reminded him of his wife, especially because of my collarbones. It was really, really awkward." That kind of thing could make people uncomfortable working with you or for you, and something not much more extreme could even lead to questions of harassment. Stay away.

Fun fact: A 2002 study from Bowling Green State University found that women are more likely than men to perceive a personal compliment in the workplace as harassment.

Assuming someone gives you an appropriate compliment at work, the right way to take it is simple: "Just say thank you," Goldstein said. "Be gracious and accept the compliment." Goldstein theorized that people have trouble accepting compliments, even at work, because they don't want to be seen as arrogant. But taking a compliment doesn't make you a braggart; it means you appreciate being appreciated.

In a working environment, taking a compliment well is not just polite; it might be crucial to your success. "Managers and bosses look for people who are good at their job and people who are good at taking feedback," Goldstein explained. "This is one of the most desirable qualities in an employee. It's a sign of confidence and competence if you can take a compliment well. If you defer a compliment, and say things like, 'Oh, I'm not that good' or 'It wasn't a big deal,' people you work with will start to believe you."

On the other hand, Goldstein said, you don't want to go looking for compliments at work. A client of hers recently told her he wanted to tell his boss about everything he'd accomplished on a project because he wanted the boss to recognize and say what a good job he'd done. But that was fishing for a compliment, a big no-no at work and in life. "No one likes to be manipulated into giving a compliment," Goldstein said. "No manager, no boss, no person." Her advice: "Do your job well and be visible, don't hide—but never fish for compliments. Sometimes it's a matter of reframing your accomplishments. Just present what you did and don't expect any kudos in return."

Make complimenting your coworkers, bosses, and employees a habit—something you do often, as long as it's sincere. "You can be a hero in your organization by becoming a picker-upper person," Glenn Van Ekeren wrote. "Make it a way of life rather than a periodic or one-time event."

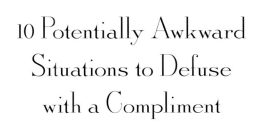

10 Potentially Awkward Situations to Defuse with a Compliment

1. You walk into a party and don't know a soul

Even the most gregarious people get uncomfortable about the idea of walking into a room full of strangers and trying to socialize. A compliment can be a great icebreaker. Head to the bar, scope out the scene while you get a cocktail, and then—without interrupting an intense tête-à-tête—approach someone you'd like to talk to and lead with, "That's a great bag" or, "Fantastic tie." From there, follow up by introducing yourself and chatting about how you both know the host.

2. The beginning of a blind date

Even when you've had a pre-date cocktail (or three), the first few moments of a blind date are uncomfortable at best—whether you're

nervous as heck staring across the table at an uberhottie or wondering why, why, *why* you agreed to do this instead of curling up in your PJs and catching up on TiVo. It helps to remember that the person across the table from you probably isn't feeling a whole lot more relaxed, so put him at ease—and make things easier for yourself, too—by paying a compliment as soon as you can think of a sincere one. The automatic "You look great," is fine, but you don't know what he usually looks like, so try to make it a little more specific. Maybe something like, "You have great taste in restaurants" or, "Your e-mail today cracked me up" or, going back to the appearance thing, "I really like that shirt." Don't dwell on it, just say it; move along to the whole get-to-know-you portion of the program. And order another cocktail.

3. The end of a blind date

If the evening went well, a compliment with a flirty overtone—"If I'd known you were going to be this funny and good-looking, I would have asked John to set us up months ago"—lets your date know you're intrigued without totally hanging you out on the "So, when can we get together again?" limb. And if there were zero sparks, a simple, platonic compliment (like "I enjoyed meeting you" followed by "Thanks for a nice night") gives you a way to end things gracefully without falling into the "Um, I'll, well, I'll call you" trap.

4. You don't remember someone you've met before

Oops. We've all been there, greeting someone we *think* we're meeting for the first time with an enthusiastic "Nice to meet you," only to be told, "Uh, we've met." (Making an effort to remember names, which I talk about on page 73, can help you avoid this unpleasant scenario). Though the gaffe might make you feel silly, don't dwell on that. Think about it from the perspective of the person you forgot, who might be embarrassed that he didn't make much of an impression on you. If possible, try to make him feel memorable and important with a compliment. Chat with him a bit and get to know him, and find a reason to tell him something nice like: "You have an intriguing job" or, "I'd love to hear you play the guitar" or even laugh sincerely at a good story he tells.

5. Someone you've met before doesn't remember *you*

Now you're the one on the receiving end of a blank stare from someone you've been introduced to already, and it doesn't feel very good. But this time, don't focus on that. (Just think: The person's lapse in memory wasn't intentional, and he's obviously not very good at the basics of social interaction. His problem, not yours.) The faux pas perpetrator may feel uncomfortable, but you can eliminate his discomfort—and make yourself someone he will definitely remember this time—by paying a quick, sweet compliment.

6. You've said something not-so-sweet about someone whose best friend or girlfriend or mother is in the room

Generally speaking, it's a good idea to refrain from saying mean things about other people. Why waste the time and negative energy when there are so many excellent compliments to be paid? I know, I know, occasionally, we all slip and let something catty escape our lips. Try not to do that anymore. But if you do, and you suddenly realize who overheard you, don't backpedal or spout apologies. Drop it immediately and try to follow up the insult with at least one sincerely kind, out-loud remark about the object of your affront. It might not save the day completely but it could leave those around you feeling less offended.

7. A business meeting

Make your potential client or boss feel great with a compliment near the beginning of a meeting. She might soften up a bit, which could help you feel at ease before you make a presentation or go to bat for your new plan. Focus on the professional—compliment a recent business initiative, marketing strategy, product launch, or the latest quarterly results. Express your admiration succinctly and move on to the topic at hand.

8. A job interview

A specific compliment—strictly professional, of course—during a job interview can demonstrate your knowledge about a company and the person who's interviewing you in a way that makes the interviewer feel important. Comment favorably on an article he recently published or

a speech he made or about recent changes in the company that he was responsible for. Have a few potential compliments ready to go before the interview, and slide one in if and when it doesn't feel forced. Yes, this requires a little advance research. But if you want this job, you should be doing that anyway. If you're the one doing the interviewing, consider paying a compliment to the nervous job applicant. You've seen her resume and there's a reason she's in your office, so compliment her early on. This could help her to relax and give you a better sense of who she really is—and whether she's right for the job.

9. You run into an ex who jilted you

Ideally, you'll be sporting your best see-you-in-hell look. But even if you're in workout clothes and still sweating after a gym session, you'll look fabulous if you act friendly, smile, and pay a quick (not too personal) compliment. Even if there's a little lingering bitterness, choke it down and say—calmly and without tears—something like, "You look great" or, "I heard about your promotion; that's terrific news." You'll come across as confident, sane, and over it.

10. You run into an ex whom you jilted

Though you may feel uncomfortable, remember that he is feeling worse about this interaction than you are. Be nice and say something complimentary—but not flirtatious, in case he's still carrying a torch. (And let's be honest. He probably is.) Ask him how his latest road race or triathlon went, and praise him for his strong finish. Give him a chance to brag a little and offer your congratulations. Hey, he doesn't get to have you anymore—he could use a little kindness.

Little Compliments

OFTEN YOU DON'T need to say anything to pay someone a fantastic compliment. Smiling, remembering someone's name, giving a thoughtful gift, dressing nicely when you see someone or attend an occasion they are hosting, trusting someone with a secret or a responsibility, asking someone's opinion, taking the time to send a handwritten letter just because, with no agenda—these are all small yet compelling compliments that leave the recipient (and the giver) feeling good.

As Samuel Johnson wrote, "We every day see men of eminence followed with all the obsequiousness of dependence, and courted with all the blandishments of flattery, by those who want nothing from them but professions of regard, and who think themselves liberally rewarded by a bow, a smile, or an embrace."

Here's how to pay a subtle compliment—in some cases, without saying a word.

Smile

This one is *so* easy—and at the same time, it's a challenge for many of us. Smiling sincerely at someone, whether she is a friend or a stranger, lets her know she is welcome and that you are open to knowing her. And when we don't do it—when we scowl or look blankly—we can hurt others' feelings without realizing it. I recently went to a yoga class at a studio I'd never visited before. I meant to arrive early to scope out a good spot but, like always, I got there in the nick of time, and a mass of yogis was milling around jockeying for position. I couldn't quite tell how we were supposed to position ourselves in relation to the teacher (every class has its routine) and asked another woman, who appeared to be a regular, for guidance. She stared at me coldly (*no* smile), shrugged her shoulders, and turned away. I felt like I'd been slapped. And I wondered if I had drool running down the side of my face or something. Another woman saw that transaction, came over with a big smile, and quickly pointed out where the teacher would be.

Her information was helpful, but with her smile she paid me a nice compliment at a moment when I needed it—she made me feel like I was worthy and welcome and like she was glad to have me there. In all likelihood, woman number one didn't mean to be bitchy, but was just uncertain about what to tell me. Maybe she would have felt silly smiling at me, someone she didn't know. I'm not sure. All I know is the snub felt terrible; the smile felt great. Please don't be afraid to smile.

When we greet friends and loved ones with a generous, enthusiastic grin, we tell them—without a word—that we are happy to see them. And everyone takes that as a compliment, whether or not they acknowledge it consciously. So be free with the smiles whenever you see someone who makes you happy.

Fun fact: Smiling is good for you—it has been shown to reduce stress, boost the immune system, lower blood pressure, increase your chances of getting a promotion at work, and make you look younger and more attractive.

Don't be afraid that smiling makes you vulnerable or puts you at risk for being taken less seriously. On the contrary: A sincere smile demonstrates that you are relaxed, self-confident, and trusting. And sharing even the slightest hint of trust is a compliment. Smiling is an incredibly easy way to make someone else's day a little better.

Remember names

If you meet someone, and five minutes later he's already forgotten your name—even though people do this all the time—it's a little insulting. If, on the other hand, someone you met briefly *remembers* your name days or weeks or months later, that's a compliment. According to Dale Carnegie, "The average person is more interested in his or her own name than in all the other names on earth put together. Remember that name and call it easily, and you have paid a subtle and very effective compliment."

When Andre Agassi retired from tennis, magazine writers and sportscasters interviewed his fellow players and others from the tennis world. Pretty much everyone talked about how much they like and admire him, and I was struck by the number of times people cited the fact that he remembered *everyone's* name. Ball boys, locker room attendants, and players new to the tour all appreciated this and felt honored that Agassi thought they were important enough to remember. For the rest of us non–Grand Slam winners, remembering names is still a simple compliment we can pay to those we meet.

So when someone tells you her name, listen. Make a note of it. If you don't quite understand how to pronounce it, ask her to repeat it right away. (That is not offensive, and it's much better than never saying her name.) Then repeat it to yourself whenever she says something and use it again the very next time you speak to her. Write it down if you have to. Figure out a way to remember it and take the time to use it. Most of us are barely scratching the surface of our brain's capacity—you've got room for a few more names in there.

Give thoughtful gifts

Expensive, flashy gifts aren't nearly as complimentary as thoughtful ones—which is nice because it means you can pay someone a great compliment without dropping a lot of cash. If you think enough of someone to get her a gift, think just a little bit more about what she would *really* like. The compliment is in the thought that goes into the gift (hey, it *is* the thought that counts) and the remembrance of what's meaningful to the recipient. When someone chooses a thoughtful gift for me, it tells me she cares enough about me and is interested enough in me to take note of what I like, need, or appreciate. It tells me I'm important to her.

My friend Kerri is the best gift-giver I know. And it's not because she's especially extravagant. Every single gift she gives me is a small compliment because it always tells me that she thinks I'm special. One year, for my birthday, she hunted down an old black-and-white photograph and a poem that related to an important conversation we had. She put them together in a simple, beautiful frame. Only I understood exactly what it meant, and it made me cry (in a good way—and I'm not a crier). It didn't cost her much money, but it meant more to me than anything else she could have given.

Even if you're just picking up a hostess gift, if you actually *like* said hostess, pay her a compliment by considering her proclivities and choosing something she will enjoy. Does she love sauvignon blanc? Get that and skip the chardonnay. Is she making an effort to live green? No disposable cocktail napkins—opt for a reusable set in organic cotton or linen. She'll be flattered (and your gift won't go to waste).

> Get not your friends by bare compliments, but by giving them sensible tokens of your love.
>
> —Socrates

I almost always like getting flowers, but they really feel like a compliment when someone thinks to pick up, say, a bouquet of local, organic flowers from the farmers market (taking into consideration my environmental streak) or a few stems of hydrangeas (because they know how much I love Nantucket). On the other hand, my friend Carrie is allergic to most flowers; a bouquet of perfect long-stemmed roses does nothing but make her sneeze. But a pretty assortment of leaves and berries that won't make her eyes water tells her that the giver really cares about her and doesn't want her to have a sneezing fit. That might seem like a small thing, but it's a big compliment.

We love flattery, even though we are not deceived by it, because it shows that we are of importance enough to be courted. Something like that pleasure, the flowers give us: what am I to whom these sweet hints are addressed?
—Ralph Waldo Emerson

Use the thoughtful gifts you're given

When someone takes the time to choose a gift for you, pay a quiet compliment back to her by *using* it. If someone brings a wonderful bottle of wine to your dinner party, consider pouring it that night and letting your guests know where it came from—or let the giver know what special occasion you'll be saving it for. When a friend gives you a book she knows you'll love, tell her about your favorite chapter as soon as you've read it. When a long-distance friend sends a housewarming gift, write a thank-you note that explains just where you'll put the picture frame or how much your guests loved the platter when you used it at a cocktail party.

Recently, when I was getting near the end of being pregnant and pretty much uncomfortable all the time (but still wanting to look vaguely cute), my husband picked out a set of adorable flannel pajamas for me. He was nervous about making any sartorial decision on my behalf, so I know he took it as a compliment that I wanted to wear them right away and that I wore them often.

Write a letter for no reason

In an essay for *Town & Country*'s "Social Graces" column, Helen Gurley Brown wrote, "Unless your arm is broken and you can't even make an X to sign your name, or you have lost your brains and decided to abandon a seriously efficient form of friend pleasing and friend making, I feel strongly you should be writing letters." To her point, writing a letter isn't difficult. But so few of us ever take the time to do it—apart from business and other practical correspondence, and thank-you notes, which are wonderful but necessary—that getting a letter from someone for no reason has decidedly become an unspoken form of compliment.

My friend Amie is really good at this. Every now and then I'll get a quick letter from her that she wrote simply to say hello or to tell me about something funny or to share an article with me. Each time I'm surprised and delighted and flattered that she was thinking about me. Just try it and see what kind of response you get. Maybe start by writing one letter a week—it doesn't have to be long or complicated—to someone you care about and see if you can make it a life-long habit.

Ask someone's opinion

When you ask someone for her opinion, you pay a compliment. You tell her that you admire her taste enough and respect her judgment and desire her input, without having to say any of those things explicitly. Ask her what shoes you should wear with your new dress, what you should make for a dinner party, or how you should handle a tough work situation. Whatever. If there's someone you think might give good counsel, ask her. You don't necessarily need to heed her advice to the letter, but in addition to being a compliment, asking another person's opinion just might teach you something. As Ralph Waldo Emerson said, "Every man I meet is my superior in some way. In that, I learn of him."

Dress for the occasion

I had a book party last year that I was very excited about, and I put some time and thought into choosing an outfit. But that's to be expected—it was my book party. When one of my good friends called me to talk about what *she* was going to wear, I took it as a compliment. She was looking forward to the party almost as much as I was, she understood what a big deal it was for me, and she wanted to make sure she had on a great outfit for it. This might seem like a superficial way to pay a compliment—image isn't everything, after all, and who cares what you wear? But it's not about the labels. It's about putting time, thought, and care into your appearance for someone else's sake. Doing this is a compliment whether you're going to someone's book launch, her wedding, her baby shower, or a dinner party she's hosting. Excessive formality isn't required, but a little effort on your part sends a message that you appreciate her.

Make friends feel at home

According to the English novelist Edward Bulwer-Lytton (perpetrator of such truisms as "The pen is mightier than the sword"), "To dispense with ceremony is the most delicate mode of conferring a compliment." And that is no truism—it's true. When we let down our guard and relax around others, especially when we invite them into our homes, we allow them to relax around us. We let them know we trust them and feel good with them. The hostess with the mostest doesn't walk around with a stick up her you-know-what and make guests feel like they need to be on their best behavior. She's relaxed, and she gives signals to her guests that she likes them, that they are welcome, and that she's glad they came.

There are dozens of other little ways we can compliment people without making an overt comment. Every time we are thoughtful—every time we return a phone call promptly,

RSVP to a party right away (and don't back out!), do a small favor without expecting anything in return—we let people know we care about them. And that is a fantastic little compliment that no one can ever get too often.

Compliments for Kids

As you hone your complimenting skills, don't forget to pay compliments to the little people in your life. From the time we are very young, sincere compliments can help to shape and encourage us. I don't know if I'd be a writer now if my mom hadn't praised the stories I wrote when I was little and told me I should keep it up. She also told me, after reading an essay I wrote in high school, "You're a good writer." Even if she was the only one who thought so, she meant it and shared it with me. And I appreciate it. (Thanks, Mom.)

Young children love to be praised by their parents, who are the most important people in their worlds. They crave compliments and the sense of approval that comes with them. Being praised—when it's deserved—by a grown-up gives a kid a sense of validation and self-worth.

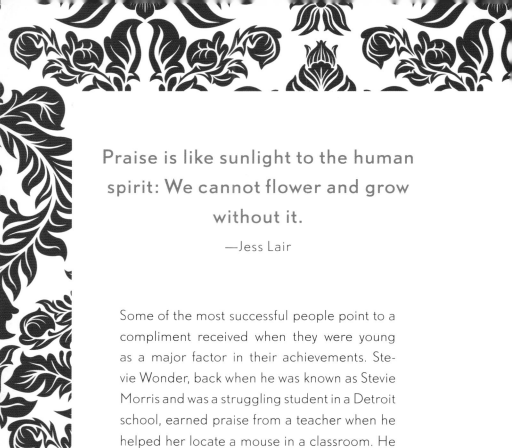

> Praise is like sunlight to the human spirit: We cannot flower and grow without it.
>
> —Jess Lair

Some of the most successful people point to a compliment received when they were young as a major factor in their achievements. Stevie Wonder, back when he was known as Stevie Morris and was a struggling student in a Detroit school, earned praise from a teacher when he helped her locate a mouse in a classroom. He couldn't see, but she told him how fantastic his hearing was. Being appreciated like that was a new experience for him, and he has said it changed his life.

A young Charles Dickens was toiling away pasting labels to bottles in a factory when an editor first praised and accepted a story he wrote (this was after he'd received many, many rejections). The sliver of encouragement

gave him the confidence to pursue one of the greatest literary careers in history. Later in the nineteenth century, H. G. Wells was in a similar situation, working fourteen hours per day at a menial job, when he received a letter from a former teacher telling him how intelligent he was and what great things he could accomplish. This compliment has been credited with helping to transform his life from one of great despair to one of enormous success.

Many of the friends I talked to about compliments cited those received when they were young as some of the most important and memorable. "Looking back on it," my cousin-in-law Chuck told me, "nothing meant more to me at a specific time in my life than a comment from my middle school football coach. When I made a really big hit in football practice as a seventh grader, my coach yelled, 'Looks like we got ourselves a football player!' As a thirteen-year-old in southern Ohio, nothing could have felt better." Chuck went on to captain his nationally-ranked collegiate lacrosse team. The early praise of his athletic ability might well have been a motivating factor.

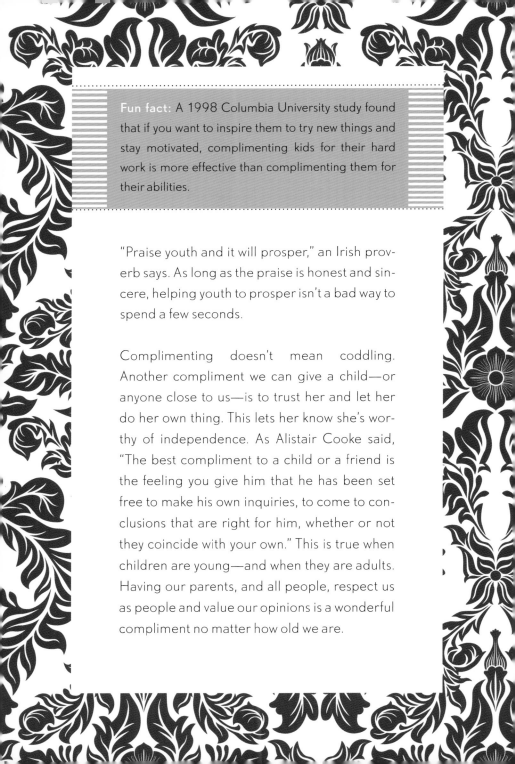

Fun fact: A 1998 Columbia University study found that if you want to inspire them to try new things and stay motivated, complimenting kids for their hard work is more effective than complimenting them for their abilities.

"Praise youth and it will prosper," an Irish proverb says. As long as the praise is honest and sincere, helping youth to prosper isn't a bad way to spend a few seconds.

Complimenting doesn't mean coddling. Another compliment we can give a child—or anyone close to us—is to trust her and let her do her own thing. This lets her know she's worthy of independence. As Alistair Cooke said, "The best compliment to a child or a friend is the feeling you give him that he has been set free to make his own inquiries, to come to conclusions that are right for him, whether or not they coincide with your own." This is true when children are young—and when they are adults. Having our parents, and all people, respect us as people and value our opinions is a wonderful compliment no matter how old we are.

Lovely Compliments

MEANINGFUL COMPLIMENTS come in all shapes and sizes. They don't have to be grand and sweeping; more often, they are straightforward and related to some element of everyday life. Someone doesn't need to win a Pulitzer Prize to deserve a compliment or to feel like she can accept one. And those everyday compliments stick with people, perhaps more than the big ones do.

While working on this book, I polled more than one hundred friends, friends of friends, and family members to get their input on all things compliment-related. Most of them remembered a few very sweet compliments that they were eager to relate. (The other thing everyone wanted to weigh in on is how you can tell when compliments are insincere. There's much more about that on page 119, but here's the deal: People know when you're faking, so don't do it.)

I mention lots of these lovely compliments throughout this book; here's an eclectic sampling of compliments (received by people I know and a few famous folks) that seem especially delightful to me.

My mother-in-law, Lee, told me, "Probably the nicest compliment I've ever received is 'What wonderful sons you have raised' or variations of that praise, and these are frequent. I have never doubted their sincerity or had trouble accepting them. I always respond with thanks." I happen to agree with that compliment about her sons—I married one of them, and he is pretty awesome. I also have no doubt that those who paid her this compliment were sincere. A compliment to a proud mother about her parenting skills or her children is always received well.

My friend Katie told me that one of her favorite compliments came from *her* mother-in-law, who told Katie (after the birth of Katie's daughter, Evelyn) that she thinks Katie is a wonderful mother. Katie will probably never forget that, and it gave her valuable confidence early in motherhood.

Compliments to a woman's maternal skills are always lovely. Virginia Woolf once told the composer Dame Ethel Smith, "You are, I believe, one of the kindest women, one of the best balanced, with that maternal quality that of all others I need and adore."

When it's true, my friend Meg tells people, "I love spending time with you." She said it's always appreciated. (She is correct—she has told me that, and it means a lot.)

Come home, for 'tis dull living without you.

—Hester Piozzi to Samuel Johnson

"The nicest compliment I received was from my neighbor," my friend Beth told me. "She said, 'You are a great neighbor and you make me feel like I'm part of your family.' It meant a lot to me because she and her family moved down to North Carolina from New York last year and were having some trouble feeling comfortable with the area. It wasn't until we really started to get to know each other that she told me how she felt."

The archduchess of Württemberg told her friend Lady William Russell, "When I came here my first thoughts were of you, my dear and excellent friend; the joy of finding you again was the warmest feeling I know."

Julia Wedgewood, the writer, told her friend Robert Browning, "My friendship with you was—is—the greatest blessing of my life. I think I need not say whether every word of yours is precious to me."

"The nicest compliment I can remember is someone saying that my pasta sauce belongs in a restaurant," my sister-in-law Jenny said. Jenny does make a mouth-watering pasta sauce and that specific compliment, focused on a unique and specific talent and skill, made her feel great.

When Lyndon Johnson was deciding whether or not to run for president in 1964, thinking much of the country—and the press—opposed him, Lady Bird Johnson bolstered his confidence with a letter containing these powerful compliments: "Beloved—You are as brave a man as Harry Truman—or FDR—or Lincoln. You can go on to find some peace, some achievement amidst all the pain. You have been strong, patient, determined beyond any words of mine to express . . . I know you are as brave as any of the thirty-five. I love you always . . . " Even incumbent presidents need to be reminded that their loved ones admire them; it worked, and he ran (and won in a landslide, by the way, in case your U.S. history is rusty).

"Someone in my husband's family whom I am not particularly close to recently said that she admired me because I seem to be very comfortable with myself, that I just do my own thing," my friend Tita said. "That really gave me a sense of pride and validation, to know that as I am approaching my forties, I have really come into my own, that I have found a place of acceptance of myself, that I am no longer that twenty-year-old yearning to belong somewhere or to someone." This kind of compliment is tough to fake, and Tita felt the sincerity and appreciated it on a deep and substantive level.

"When my kids say 'I love you' spontaneously and sincerely," my friend Carrie said, "to me, that is a huge compliment." The joy she takes from hearing that stems at least in part from the fact that she knows her kids—ages three and four—truly mean it. Utter sincerity makes any compliment special. And a compliment from a child is nothing but a delight. You can't (and should not) angle for it—but when it comes, it's priceless.

I love you because you're you.

—Michel Eyquem de Montaigne

One of the nicest compliments I have ever received came recently, from my husband, when we were talking about this book. I asked him about the nicest compliment he'd ever received. He thought about it and told me it was when I said yes when he asked me to marry him. (Awww.) I'm not sure if he was trying to pay a compliment or not, but it definitely *was* a compliment. And I loved it.

Put it in writing: Letter from Nathaniel Hawthorne to his wife, Sophia:

Unspeakably Belovedest,

Thy letter has just been handed to me. It was most comfortable to me, because it gives such a picture of thy life with the children. I could see the whole family of my heart before my eyes, and could hear you all talking together...

I want thee so much. Thou art the only person in the world that ever was necessary to me. Other people have occasionally been more or less agreeable; but I think I was always more at ease alone than in anybody's company, till I knew thee. And now I am only myself when thou art within my reach. Thou art an unspeakably beloved woman...

If I write any more, it would only be to express more lovings and longings; and as they are impossible to express, I may as well close.

Thy Husband

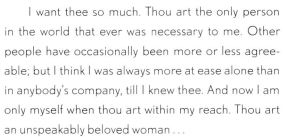

15 No-Fail Compliments

If you pay one of these compliments sincerely, you can't go wrong.

1. You look stunning.

2. You have wonderful taste.

3. You made your home beautiful.

4. You're in great shape.

5. Your daughter/son is charming.

6. You are an excellent mother (or father).

7. You're an amazing _____.
(Fill in the blank with whatever is appropriate—mother, father, runner, pianist, party planner, chef, painter, doctor, butcher, baker, candlestick-maker—as long as it will ring true and mean something to the recipient.)

8. I've learned so much from you.

9. Your opinion is important to me.

10. You inspire me.

11. You're fantastic in bed. (Please use this only when you have explicit and recent knowledge of said bedroom ability; otherwise it's creepy.)

12. You're doing terrific work.

13 I can't see wait to see you.

14. It doesn't matter what we do—I just want to be with you.

15. I love you. (Of course, you should use this one only with someone you truly love—not on a second date. Someone who is also in love with you will never, ever tire of hearing it.)

Compliment vs. Complement: A Very Short Chapter

THIS IS A BOOK about compliments, not a book about usage or spelling, and not about complements, either. I suspect most of you know the difference between *compliment* and *complement*. If so, please turn past the next page, and thank you. If not, bear with me for a moment. Every now and then, I see the words compliment and complement misused and interchanged. This is a pet peeve of mine.

(Don't even get me started on stationery and stationary.) So here, for your reading pleasure, from *The New Merriam-Webster Dictionary,* are the definitions of *compliment* and *complement.*

[1] compliment *noun* **1:** an expression of approval or courtesy; a flattering remark **2:** best wishes

[2] compliment *verb* to pay a compliment to

(*Example: Thank you for saying you like this book. That's a nice compliment.*)

[1] complement *noun* **1:** a quantity needed to make a thing complete **2:** full quantity, number, or amount

[2] complement *verb* to be complementary to; fill out

(*Example: This book is a nice complement to general books on etiquette.*)

Random Acts of Compliment

SOMETIMES, I THINK I prefer compliments from strangers to those from acquaintances. A stranger—most likely—has no ulterior motive, no reason to suck up, and nothing to gain by complimenting you. And receiving an unexpected compliment from a complete stranger can be a serious mood booster. I got one recently in the midst of a long and miserable day, and it was transformative.

After a cross-country plane ride full of such pleasures as a screaming, whining four-year-old, a middle seat next to a sneezing row-mate who liked elbowing his way six inches over the arm rest into my personal space, and a forty-minute delay in connecting to the jetway after landing, I waited in an endless taxi line as the sky dumped buckets of rain. I arrived at my hotel an hour after check-in time only to learn that my room wasn't ready and wouldn't be for another hour. I had a dinner to get to, and I wanted a shower first. But apparently, that wasn't happening. So I took my bag to the lobby restroom, waited for a wave of nausea to pass (I was ten weeks pregnant—in other words, feeling sick and bloated and not yet telling anyone why), and navigated my way out of my airplane clothes and into a reasonably sassy dress—outside of my typical LBD comfort zone—that didn't call attention to my puffy midsection.

Fun fact: Most people give compliments to someone of an age and status close to their own. (But that doesn't mean you shouldn't compliment someone who is older or younger than you!)

I had thrown my rain-soaked hair into a tight ponytail and was deciding whether to curl up in a little nauseous ball on the floor or put on mascara when another hotel guest came into the bathroom. She was young and sweet, and I will love her forever because she stopped short and quickly assessed me and my dress. She said, with a sincere smile, "Well, you look *lovely!*" Ha. Until that moment, I was feeling anything but. Maybe she sensed my despair. Regardless of what prompted her, she fixed my outlook in a nanosecond. Suddenly, I felt better—maybe even lovely, or as close to lovely as I was going to feel under those circumstances. I stood up straighter, applied mascara *and* some lip shimmer, and proceeded to my dinner with a little spring in my step (along with an umbrella borrowed from the hotel in hand).

So please, don't be afraid to compliment a stranger if you feel the urge. Tell her you love her dress or her shoes or that she has great taste in bags or books or flowers or whatever she's carrying. Keep it simple and brief, and expect nothing in return. Oh, and don't make it too personal. You don't want to scare anyone with too-close-for-comfort comments like "I love the smell of your deodorant" or "What great underwear—those are such tight pants and there's no VPL."

My friend Julie recalls receiving an over-the-top-verging-on-frightening compliment from someone she didn't know: "I was walking down the street and a man pulled his car over to tell me I had the nicest legs," she said. "He went on and on about how they were so toned, so fit, so strong and tan, in such great shape. At first I was flattered, but then I got totally repulsed and just wanted to use my toned legs to run right out of there."

My friend Regan remembered a customer from when she was waiting tables telling her, "You walk smooth as a cat. Do you do any athletics?" (Seriously. He said that. Um, huh?) Her response, she said, "was to glide smoothly away, as far as I could get."

Be sincere and enthusiastic but dial down the content—and please, be normal—when you're praising a stranger.

Put it in writing: Fan letter to George Harrison, via John Lennon:

Dear John,

    Please forward this letter to George.

    I think you are wonderful too.

Dearest Darling Beatle George,

    I was very disappointed when you came to the U.S.A. and didn't come to see me. You don't know what you missed. I'm really a beautiful doll. I am 5'3" tall and slender and very good looking. I would make some Beatle a very lovely wife. Since I consider you the prettiest one, I'm giving you first choice. If you decide that you will be my lucky husband, then I will know that not only are you pretty, but also very intelligent.

    Every night before I go to sleep, I say, Goodnight, Georgie. I love you. Yeah, yeah, yeah!

    So think it over my love and give me your answer. If you are stupid enough to decline my offer, forward this letter to Ringo and Paul. Forget about John, he's married, you know.

    I think you are the most.

    All my love,

    Your Donna

Praise in Absentia

If you have a compliment to pay, but the object of your admiration isn't present, say what you're thinking anyway.

The compliment might get back to whomever you were complimenting. You have no control over whether that will happen, but if it does, you just gave a sweet treat to someone—in the future. As *The Amy Vanderbilt Complete Book of Etiquette* reminds us, "It is particularly satisfying to receive a secondhand compliment . . . a secondhand compliment can mean much more than if you heard it directly."

"It feels really nice to hear that someone said something nice about you," my friend Carrie said, "but not have them telling it directly to you. Like if one friend tells you that another friend said such and such about you, somehow that means it is even more sincere, because why would they offer that kind of nice comment insincerely if you're not even there?"

While you're at it, remember that a compliment behind someone's back is a good thing but an insult is not. Neither is malicious gossip. As Kate Spade wrote in her book *Manners*, "Gossiping is as reckless as riding in a car without a seat belt. Buckle up, button up, zip it, sshhhh." The writer Molly Haskell explained in the essay "What's So Good About Gossip?" that she wrote for *Town & Country*'s "Social Graces" column, "You don't want to betray your best friend or be the bearer of tidings that will devastate the listener, wreck a marriage, or destroy a reputation . . . you want to be someone who, even in a society with few boundaries, knows how to respect privacy when the occasion demands it."

Back to compliments: If you *hear* a compliment about someone else when she isn't around, share it with her later. Don't keep it to yourself. According to our friend Amy Vanderbilt, "Passing on a compliment is a mark of generosity that can't help but please."

(There's no need to pass on insults or gossip, of course. But remember, if you're the perpetrator of said gossip, someone else may spill it. Keep that in mind before you spout something mean, and as my mom—probably yours too—would say, if you can't say something nice, don't say anything at all.)

My most brilliant achievement was my ability to persuade my wife to marry me.

—Winston Churchill

Age-old question: Should your compliment include a reference to age? Maybe—if you're careful and don't over- or under-estimate someone's age in the wrong direction. People who are sensitive about their age would probably love a sincere compliment that suggests they look or seem younger than they actually are.

Most likely, just about any woman over the age of twenty-five (and any man over the age of thirty) is flattered by those compliments, whether or not they are particularly sensitive about their age. Of course, younger people usually just want to look more grown up. No seven-year-old I've ever met thinks it a compliment to be told he looks like he's five or six; ditto, an eighteen-year-old who's told she looks fifteen.

Also, being told you look good *for your age* isn't likely to leave anyone feeling especially swell. So don't use that one.

Just Take It: Accepting Compliments with Grace and Style

EVEN WHEN A COMPLIMENT is completely sincere and makes us feel great, we often don't know what to do with it. And sometimes our reaction kind of ruins it.

I still cringe when I think back to my response to a compliment on a date—a first date—with someone I had a bit of a crush on. A few minutes into the thing, over cocktails at a swanky Boston bar, he told me I looked great and that he couldn't believe I'd run a half-marathon that day (which I had, and which he knew because it had pushed back our start time by a few hours). Instead of smiling and thanking him and moving on, some combination of nerves and awkwardness inspired me to tell him that in fact I wasn't looking all that good. I explained that I'd worn a new sports bra during the race and it had rubbed off swaths of skin under my armpits—which I proceeded to show him.

A compliment is a gift, not to be thrown away carelessly, unless you want to hurt the giver.

—Eleanor Hamilton

Chafed, scabbed skin really isn't something you want to be sharing with people you don't know well. (Maybe not even with people you *do* know well.) Especially not in public, and certainly not when there are a whole lot of beautiful people around. It just doesn't go over well. He was taken aback—he might have even visibly recoiled—and he excused himself to go to the restroom, on the way back from which he stopped a few times to chat with cute, non-chafed women. Yeah, we didn't go out again.

Not knowing how to respond to a compliment is common. According to *The Amy Vanderbilt Complete Book of Etiquette*, "many of us, especially women, were taught not to preen. So we feel self-conscious and act disingenuous when paid a compliment."

But as my friend Julie said, a grown woman (and a grown man, for that matter) should know how to accept a compliment. When someone gives you a compliment, all you have to do—and all you should do—is say thank you, with as much sincerity and warmth as your complimenter used while giving it. That's it.

"It's not conceited to accept a compliment," wrote Lizzie Post, Emily Post's great-great-granddaughter, in *How Do You Work This Life Thing? Advice for the Newly Independent on Roommates, Jobs, Sex, and Everything That Counts.* And she was right. Accepting it (briefly) and moving on is, in fact, the only way to respond. But so many people do anything but that. Here are a few tips to help you recognize the typical ways we refuse compliments—and to help you remember simply to say thanks, or something similar, with a smile and enthusiasm.

Fun fact: According to a 1990 study published in the journal *Language and Society* (and many other studies), women are more likely than men to receive compliments.

Avoid explaining away a compliment or giving the complimenter *way* more information than he wanted

We've all tried this one. When someone compliments me on something I'm wearing, I usually tell that person how old it is or that I got it on sale. I've even done that when wearing the rare pair of expensive shoes that I paid retail price for. Not that it matters—if they like something I'm wearing and tell me, they are complimenting me on my taste, not the size of my wallet. There are plenty of hideous, expensive garments out there. And unless they specifically ask where I got something, they probably don't want shopping tips, either.

My friend Deb does the same thing when she gets a compliment. "Someone complimented me on a pair of earrings I was wearing," she said. "I immediately told her, 'They're not real. They're from Banana Republic.' My mom overheard me and begged me just to say thank you next time." And my friend Emily does it too. "I usually feel like I have to follow up or explain something related to the compliment," she said. "Say someone were to compliment me on my shirt—I thank them, and then say something about where it came from, like 'I just picked it up on sale' or 'So-and-so gave it to me for my birthday. . . .'" But, she said, she'd like to stop doing that. "When people give compliments, they aren't looking for that information."

Think about how you would feel if you complimented someone's outfit and she dismissed it by saying it was cheap or old or awful. You might feel silly for having paid the compliment or wonder if she thought you had questionable taste. Why do that to someone who simply wants to say something nice to you?

Don't dismiss or wave off a compliment

After I ran the Boston Marathon last year, a friend and fellow runner complimented me on my time. I was disappointed with the way I'd finished and, in my pouty mood, I not only ruined what should have been a triumphant afternoon, I also forgot that my time was about the same as her personal best. When I blew off her compliment and said it hadn't been a good race, she might have perceived that I was insulting *her* time as well as my own. She didn't say anything, but she might well have been offended. Even if you don't agree with a compliment, consider the giver's point of view and don't devalue what she says or what she thinks.

In a much less rude way, my friend Carrie also tends to dismiss compliments. "If someone says, 'Wow, you're doing a great job with those kids,' I'll say, 'Well, we're just surviving,'" she explained. "Or if someone tells me I'm smart, I'll say 'Not really, I just have people fooled.'" Though she means well, she *could* be putting the complimenter in the uncomfortable position of trying to convince her that the compliment is valid.

> A refusal of praise is a desire to be praised twice.
>
> —François De La Rochefoucauld

My friend Emily explained that she dismisses compliments when she doesn't agree with them. She delivered her second baby recently, and when people told her she looked great soon afterwards—which she did; she's gorgeous—she denied it and shied away from simply saying thank you, "because I just didn't think it was true." But the people saying it probably *did* think it was true.

When people compliment us, and we respond with a dismissal or a self-deprecating comment, it's like returning a gift we didn't like. Actually, it's worse, because when someone gives you a gift you don't like, rarely do you toss it back in his or her face. (I've only done that once, when my now-husband gave me a Cincinnati Bengals T-shirt for my birthday because I thought it was his way of telling me we were breaking up. I'm a Patriots fan, you see, and I was hoping for something a wee bit more personal. I won't go into the details, but as it turned out he meant well, and I felt horrible later.)

Emily said she can accept a compliment when it's a comment on how cute her kids are, a sentiment she shares. What she needs to do—and what we all need to do—is accept even the compliments we don't agree with. And, if they come from a trustworthy source, maybe even try to believe them.

On the other hand, try not to agree *too* enthusiastically

Although, as Lizzie Post said, it's not conceited to accept a compliment, there's no need to get bragadocious. Saying thank you is one thing; saying "I know, it's true, and you know what else?" is entirely another. It might well come across as conceited if you try to expand on the compliment, and you could make the giver regret saying what she said. I speak from experience here: One night, while we were lying in bed, I told my husband that he had great eyelashes. (He does: they're long and dark and they go perfectly with his blue eyes, which I also love.) His response? "A lot of women have told me that." *Huh. Really. Please, please tell me more while we're lying in bed about what other women have said to you.* A simple thank you or smile would have been ever so much more effective. I rolled over and went to sleep. And I haven't complimented him on those eyelashes since.

Remember there is no obligation to return a compliment

This is a temptingly easy way to respond to praise, and dozens of people I talked to about this said it's how they respond to a compliment when they feel uncomfortable with it. If someone tells my friend Deb, "I love your dress," she admitted that she is quick to say, "No, I love *your* dress!" whether or not she loves the person's dress. And that's the problem with returning a compliment too quickly. What you say may not be sincere—and it probably won't come across as sincere. Plus, quickly turning a compliment around on someone doesn't give you the chance to appreciate the compliment, or the person who gave it to you.

When you reciprocate a compliment immediately, you might also lead the compliment-giver to believe that you didn't like or didn't agree with or couldn't handle the compliment—and that all you wanted to do was get rid of it.

There is not one wise man in twenty that will praise himself.

—William Shakespeare

Fish for trout, not compliments

A compliment is something we all crave but shouldn't ask for—which makes it all the more fabulous when we get a good one. "I know, indeed, of nothing more subtly satisfying and cheering than a knowledge of the real good will and appreciation of others," said the author and editor William Dean Howells, who served as president of the American Academy of Arts and Letters. "Such happiness does not come with money, nor does it flow from a fine physical state. It cannot be bought. But it is the keenest joy, after all; and the toiler's truest and best reward." And when someone does give you praise, try not to solicit more. When you receive a compliment for the main course, don't ask if the pie was tasty too. And definitely don't boast about the compliment to someone else in the hopes of additional praise.

Put it in writing: A letter from John Keats to Fanny Brawne:

Sweetest Fanny,

You fear sometimes I do not love you so much as you wish? My dear girl, I love you ever and ever and without reserve. The more I have known, the more have I lov'd. In every way—even my jealousies have been agonies of love; in the hottest fit I ever had I would have died for you. I have vexed you too much. But for love! Can I help it? You are always new. The last of your kisses was ever the sweetest, the last smile always the brightest, the last movement the gracefullest. When you pass'd my window home yesterday, I was fill'd with admiration as if I had seen you for the first time. You uttered a half complaint once that I only lov'd your beauty. Have I nothing else then to love in you but that? Do I not see a heart naturally furnish'd with wings imprison itself with me? No ill prospect has been able to turn your thoughts a moment from me. This perhaps should be as much a subject of sorrow as joy—but I will not talk of that. Even if you did not love me I could not help an entire devotion to you: how much more deeply then must I feel for you knowing you love me. My mind has been the most discontented and restless one that ever was put into a body too small for it. I never felt my mind repose upon anything with complete and undistracted enjoyment—upon no person but you. When you are in the room my thoughts never fly out of window; you always concentrate my whole senses. The anxiety shown about our loves in your last note is an immense pleasure to me; however, you must not suffer such speculations to molest you any more; nor will I any more believe you can have the least pique against me. Brown is gone out—but here is Mrs. Wylie—when she is gone I shall be awake for you. Remembrances to your mother. —Your affectionate, J. Keats.

Modesty is the only sure bait when you angle for praise.

—Lord Chesterfield

I learned that lesson in sixth grade, and never forgot it. A teacher told me privately that a little book I'd written for an assignment was the best in the class. I wanted to see if my fellow students agreed, so at lunchtime I told them what the teacher had said. Did they pile on more compliments? What do you think? They didn't speak to me for the next three days. I know that sometimes when you get a great compliment, it would be nice if the world heard about it. But it's not your job to broadcast it, and you're more likely to keep getting compliments if you don't.

If a compliment belongs to someone else, don't keep it for yourself

There is one circumstance in which it is okay to refuse a compliment: when the compliment truly isn't yours to keep and should rightfully go to someone else. If someone raves about the amazing cookies you baked (but it was actually your best friend who made them), or praises you for the unforgettable surprise party you threw (and, in fact, your sister did all the legwork and you just showed up), let the complimenter know her sentiment is valid—but the credit should go elsewhere.

Undeserved praise causes more
pangs of conscience later than
undeserved blame.

—Friedrich Nietzsche

Note: Only do this if the compliment truly should go to someone else, please. You are *not* allowed to use this as a method to avoid compliments you deserve.

Giving credit to the right person won't make you look bad at all—you'll come across as generous and honest. And try to be appreciative of the compliment anyway, acknowledging the kindness of the giver.

> Fun fact: Both men and women are more willing to accept compliments from men than from women. Compliments from women are more often met with a deflection technique.

Don't get a big head

This probably goes without saying, but just in case it doesn't, I'm going to say it. Compliments are awesome. They feel amazing. They inspire and reward us. But they shouldn't change us or make us insufferable and snotty and holierthan-thou. We shouldn't start to expect or demand them. We should enjoy them—maybe even cherish them, if they are special enough—and move on.

> The only way to escape the personal corruption of praise is to go on working.
>
> —Albert Einstein

Enjoy hearing others receive compliments—don't be offended if someone else gets a compliment and you don't

We all deserve our moment in the sun, and a compliment to someone else doesn't take anything away from you. "Let's cease thinking of our accomplishments, our wants. Let's try to figure out the other person's good points. Then," Dale Carnegie advised, "give honest, sincere appreciation."

> You can tell the character of every man when you see how he receives praise.
>
> —Seneca

10 People Who (Might) Deserve a Compliment

Complimenting friends, significant others, and colleagues is fantastic. But these aren't the only people we see every day. There are plenty of others who make our lives better, easier, and nicer. Think about who does that in your world, and consider paying them compliments. Here are a few peeps to ponder.

1. A teacher

If parents think a teacher is doing something wrong, they're likely to speak up. But what about when a teacher is doing something (or everything) *right*? It's much easier to let that slide without comment. A good teacher is a treasure—an underpaid, underappreciated treasure. Take the time to compliment the worthy teachers you encounter.

2. The nurses at your doctor's office or hospital

Docs get most of the glory while nurses do much of the work. This isn't to say a great doctor shouldn't get a compliment, but please don't overlook the nurses. They're the ones making you comfortable, taking your blood pressure, dealing with your urine samples (fun!), and doing you all sorts of other favors—probably with a lovely bedside manner—and taking little credit. Notice something specific that they do really nicely, and thank them for it. *Marlene couldn't have said it better!*

3. Your dentist

Dread, not delight, is the sensation often associated with visiting the dentist. And so most people don't lavish their dentists with compliments. But imagine how grumpy you (and your teeth) would be if you *didn't* go to the dentist. Besides, even though dental procedures aren't much fun, after a standard cleaning, you generally leave with smooth and sparkly pearly whites. Your dentist might be surprised to get a compliment from you on her gentle technique or the dazzling results—and it could be the nicest part of a day spent working in unhappy mouths.

4. The checkout clerk at a store

Next time you're waiting in line at the supermarket, notice how few people pay attention to—or even make eye contact with—the person ringing up and bagging their purchases. If that person is doing their job with efficiency and kindness, why not look at him, smile, say thank you, and maybe even pay him a little compliment?

5. The chef at your favorite restaurant

"My compliments to the chef" might sound like a cliché, but I'm guessing it's not something you say very often—if ever. Which is too bad, because at good restaurants (especially good little restaurants), the chef and his team are likely sweating over each and every plate, doing more than you know to make it perfect and delicious. If you love something, give a shout out to the kitchen. (Just don't demand that the chef leave her chaotic post to thank you in person—it might not be possible.) If you forget to compliment the chef while you're in the restaurant, do it online— post your praise via a public forum like Yelp or Chowhound so others can read about the chef's tasty menu.

6. A server at your favorite restaurant

The person who's taking your order and bringing your food and pouring your wine is working *hard*. And chances are the service has a lot to do with why you enjoy a given eatery. If your server is particularly personable, or has a knack for remembering details about your dish, or suggested the perfect bottle of wine, pay him a quick compliment about it. He probably doesn't get many of those. (FYI, this doesn't get you out of leaving a good tip.)

7. Your regular hairstylist/ manicurist/ massage therapist

If there's a personal care pro you see on a regular basis, they are probably pretty good at what they do. (Otherwise why would you keep going back to them?) Sure, you pay them and hopefully tip them, too, but a quick kind word about how much you appreciate their skill wouldn't hurt.

8. Your assistant

Are you lucky enough to have an assistant? One who is helpful and does a hundred little things for you every day? Remember, then, that you are indeed lucky. Be sure to compliment him on jobs well done—and offer little daily compliments like smiles, thanks, and occasional thoughtful tokens of your appreciation.

9 and 10. Your mom and dad

Near the top of the list of unsung heroes are many, many parents. Yes, there are exceptions, but most parents mean so well and only want the best for their offspring, from the time before those offspring are born and all the way into adulthood. Few kids think to compliment their parents (or key parental figures) while growing up, but once you're out and about and living on your own, take a moment to remember even one wonderful thing your mom or dad did as parent, and give a call to pay a compliment. I guarantee it will mean a lot. *No name mentioned here*

On Insincerity

AN INSINCERE COMPLIMENT is pretty easy to spot, if you're looking. Now, don't get all suspicious and start doubting every compliment that comes your way. And regardless of whether a compliment is for real or a big fake, your response should be pretty much the same. (A thank you and a smile. There's nothing to be gained by telling an insincere complimenter, "Oh, you don't mean that," because it's true, she doesn't. Drop it, and take her future compliments with grain of salt.)

I don't see why a man should think he is pleasing a woman enormously when he says to her a whole heap of things that he doesn't mean.

—Oscar Wilde

Body language, tone of voice, and the content of the compliment are all insincerity tip-offs. If someone doesn't look you in the eye or her voice raises an octave or there's just a general lack of feeling, she might be making up the compliment. Also, if the compliment is flimsy or irrelevant or nonspecific, don't bet your bank account on it being real. And if the person paying the compliment has an ulterior motive—she says you look pretty, then asks you to dog-sit her incontinent poodle for a week—discount the compliment, and consider declining the favor.

Here are a few of the insincerity signals that the people I polled for this book frequently mentioned:

> "If I see a person giving gratuitous compliments and using the same line all over town, I question any compliment from her that comes my way."

- "Compliments are only good if there is no angle and the intent is pure. If there is an angle, I don't believe it, and I am usually right."
- "Her tone of voice changes. She may also avoid eye contact and almost rush through it as if she does not want to really say it (but perhaps feels obligated to?)."
- "I think the tip-off is that someone is giving a compliment about something without any knowledge of the subject."
- "I know a compliment is insincere when there's too much smiling and not enough looking me in the eyes."
- "I can tell someone is faking if he isn't looking me in the eye when saying it or if he's being *too* effusive when saying it."
- "Gushing is insincere. And it makes me uncomfortable."
- "I don't believe a compliment when it is followed immediately by a request for something."
- "I doubt a compliment is real when someone is only interested in digging for a brand name. 'I like your shoes. Are they Manolos?'"
- "The source of the compliment matters. The young girls at my office do a lot of brown-nosing. When they tell me how much they like my outfit—and I know it's nothing special—I think they're full of shit." ☹ ☺ ☺ ! *Great* !

No one enjoys receiving a compliment that's obviously phony. As the playwright Wilson Mizner said, "I hate careless flattery, the kind that exhausts you in your effort to believe it."

To avoid giving an insincere compliment, remember the syllabus from Compliments 101 and start by listening well and paying attention to those around you. "If we stop thinking about ourselves for a while and begin to think of the other person's good points," Dale Carnegie wrote, "we won't have to resort to flattery so cheap and false that it can be spotted almost before it is out of the mouth."

Thanks, But No Thanks: Backhanded Compliments

WE'VE ALL HEARD THEM: comments that sound, initially, like praise but leave you questioning whether the commenter was really being nice or if there was a negative message she was trying (consciously or unconsciously) to convey.

These comments aren't nice. They're crappy. To paraphrase Alexander Pope, they are damning with faint praise. Don't say things like this to people. Even if you don't *mean* to insult someone, saying something potentially offensive could ruin her day and undermine her self-confidence for a moment or two, or longer. Give any compliment an extra-brief moment of thought to make sure it contains no negative hidden agenda. If you have a legitimate criticism or complaint, don't disguise it as a compliment. That's passive-aggressive.

Harry: You know, the first time we met, I really didn't like you that much.
Sally: I didn't like you
Harry: Yeah you did. You were just so uptight then. You're much softer now.
Sally: You know, I hate that kind of remark. It sounds like a compliment, but really it's an insult.
Harry: Okay, you're still as hard as nails.
—*When Harry Met Sally*

Mark Twain did say, "I think a compliment ought always to precede a complaint, where one is possible, because it softens resentment and insures for the complaint a courteous and gentle reception." But that's different from giving someone a backhanded compliment, because the complaint isn't buried among purportedly kind words. Besides, you should only give the kind of compliment Twain refers to if it's sincere.

And all the better if that compliment is entirely unrelated to the complaint so there's no mistaking it for a backhander.

Damn with faint praise, assent
with civil leer,
And without sneering teach the
rest to sneer;
Willing to wound, and yet afraid to strike,
Just hint a fault, and hesitate dislike . . .

—Alexander Pope

Backhanded compliments can range from almost-innocuous and petty to seriously low blows. I overheard one woman tell another at a recent cocktail party, "Your new haircut is great. It looks so much healthier than it used to look."

My friend Beth, stay-at-home mom to the adorable twins Lucy and Ferris, told me about an acquaintance of hers who dropped by for dinner and said, "Your house is so neat. I wish I had time to keep mine that neat, but I'm a working mom." *Yeah.*

12 Not Compliments

1. Your boyfriend is unbelievably hot. I'm really into him.

2. You're so much cooler than your husband.

3. Your girlfriend is a phenomenal kisser.

4. Your wife must have a great personality.

5. I've heard from so many different people that you're great in bed.

6. It's nice that you can make those shoes work three years after they went out of style.

7. It's incredible how well you've done in your career, considering it isn't a field you have a natural affinity for.

8. You're such a team player that I don't feel like I need to give you a promotion.

9. Your baby is beautiful—she doesn't look anything like you!

10. You're amazingly patient with those bratty kids of yours.

11. I think it's really cool that you just don't care what you look like.

12. You look great. You must have had a nose job (or boob job, or face lift, or Botox injection)!

If they can make penicillin out of moldy bread, they can sure make something out of you.

—Muhammad Ali, to a young boxer

Put it in writing: Excerpt from a letter from Napoleon Bonaparte to Josephine Beauharnais:

I do not love thee anymore; on the contrary, I detest thee. Thou art horrid, very awkward, very stupid, a very Cinderella. Thou dost not write me at all, thou dost not love thy husband; thou knowest the pleasures thy letters afford him, and thou dost not write him six lines of even haphazard scribble.

What do you do then all day, Madame? What matter of such importance is it that takes up your time from writing to your very good lover? What affection stifles and pushes on one side the love, the tender and constant love, which you have promised him? Who can be this marvelous, this new lover who absorbs all your instants, tyrannizes your entire days, and prevents you from being solicitous about your husband? Josephine, beware, one fine night the doors will break open and I will be there.

In truth, I am anxious, my good friend, at not receiving your news; write me quickly four pages, and say those amiable things which fill my heart with sentiment and pleasure.

Several years ago, my friend Regan, who recently started her own very successful public relations firm, had started a new job running marketing and public relations for a company. Someone asked Regan's boss (in front of Regan) how Regan was doing at her new job, and the boss replied, "Well, she's really good at organizing."

And when a distant in-law relation of mine heard that I was working on a book about compliments, she said, "That sounds like a fun little project. At least it will keep you busy."

If you pay a "compliment" that leaves the recipient with even a hint of doubt or worry about your meaning (*Was my hair split-end city before? Does she think being a full-time mom isn't hard work? Is organizing the only thing I'm good at? What, does she think my writing is just a* hobby?), it isn't a compliment at all. So don't say things like that.

Come again when you have
less time.

—Walter Sickert

If you're on the receiving end of such a "compliment," keep in mind that the negativity probably has more to do with the giver's insecurity and inability to communicate well than any failing on your part.

Some compliments are less obviously backhanded, but depending on the point of view of the recipient, they may be taken as such. Remember to think for a second about whether something that sounds like a compliment to you might be perceived differently by another.

I've had a perfectly wonderful evening. But this wasn't it.

—Groucho Marx

Put it in writing: Fan letter to Jackson Pollock:

Dear Mr. Pollock,

Just a few lines to tell you that my seven year old son Manning couldn't get over your picture Number Nine. Frankly, it looked like some of his finger-painting at school to me. However, he insisted that I write to you to tell you that he cut it out of the "Life" and put it in his scrape-book [sic]—the first painting that he has ever cut out—

He wanted you to have his picture in exchange for his copy of No. 9—which he loves.

Sincerely,

Mrs. Helen K. Sellers

The Art of Being a Woman author Véronique Vienne wrote an essay for *Town & Country*'s "Social Graces" column about "being left in limbo between sizes twelve and fourteen." In it, she explained, "Whenever someone says to me, 'You look great—have you lost weight?' I feel both flattered and frustrated . . . Compliments related to my size trigger insecurities from my childhood . . . Funny how, with just a couple of words, a large person like me can be made to feel rather small, my self-confidence shrunk to a petite size four."

He hasn't an enemy in the world, and none of his friends like him.
—Oscar Wilde about George Bernard Shaw

"Someone told me once that I look *just* like Martha Stewart," my thirty-something friend Margo recalled of being compared to the sixty-something lifestyle magnate. While that could be taken as a compliment, it could also leave a thirty-something gal wondering if she'd aged three decades overnight. Even if the giver was gaga over Martha's hotness, this kind of compliment, by comparison, tends to come across as backhanded.

My friend Lorin works in public relations, and she remembered a former client "recommending" her to another potential client by saying, "She's not a good writer, but she's the best publicist in town." Writing is a big part of any PR job (and yes, Lorin is good at it), so instead of being a ringing endorsement, this compliment left a question mark in the mind of the potential new client and certainly didn't make Lorin feel great. (Like any normal person would, she felt the negative part of the compliment outweighed the positive.) Maybe the former client thought it was funny or imagined that Lorin wouldn't care about the knock on her writing skills—but a thoughtful complimenter would realize that the first part of the remark could be taken the wrong way and would have left it out.

Just as I was finishing up this book, I received compliments that perfectly demonstrate the difference between a backhanded compliment and a welcomed compliment. At four-and-a-half-months pregnant, I had a little belly going. One woman saw me after a yoga class (in form fitting clothing) and told me, "You look good, for someone who's pregnant. I almost can't tell if you're pregnant or if you've just gained a lot of weight." *Huh. Thanks. That's really sweet of you. So I basically look like a pudge.* I smiled (weakly, admittedly) and mumbled thanks. Even when you get a backhanded compliment, that's still the right response. You just don't need to be especially enthusiastic about it.

A few days later, determined not to hide in baggy sweats, I went out for a long walk in shorts and a fitted tank top. A friend drove by, rolled down her window, and yelled out, "Hey Christie! You're looking *sexy!*" No "but," no "for a pregnant pudg-o" addendum, no comment about weight gain, nothing to make me second-guess her meaning. That's the kind of compliment I like. I believed her.

I smiled and said thanks.

And it made me feel great.

Resources (A Selected Bibliography)

These books were especially useful to me during the research and writing of *The Art of the Compliment*. If you like reading about etiquette, praise, and generally being a nice person, add these to your to-read list.

The Amy Vanderbilt Complete Book of Etiquette by **Nancy Tuckerman** and **Nancy Dunnan** (Doubleday, 1995)

Choosing Civility: The Twenty-five Rules of Considerate Conduct by **P.M. Forni** (St. Martin's Press, 2003)

Drinking Problems at the Fountain of Youth by **Beth Teitell** (HarperCollins, 2008)

Emily Post's Etiquette, 17th Edition by **Peggy Post** (HarperCollins, 2004)

Essential Manners for Men: What to Do, When to Do It, and Why by **Peter Post** (HarperCollins, 2003)

The 50 Greatest Love Letters of All Time, edited by **David Lowenherz** (Gramercy Books, 2005)

Funny Letters from Famous People, edited by **Charles Osgood** (Broadway Books, 2003)

How to Win Friends and Influence People by **Dale Carnegie** (revised edition, Simon & Schuster, 1981)

In Praise of Flattery by **Willis Goth Regier** (University of Nebraska Press, 2007)

Letters of the Century: America 1900–1999, edited by **Lisa Grunwald** and **Stephen J. Adler** (The Dial Press, 1999)

Love Letters of Great Men, edited by **Ursula Doyle** (St. Martin's Press, 2008)

Manners by **Kate Spade** (Simon & Schuster, 2004)

Modern Manners: The Thinking Person's Guide to Social Graces, edited by **Thomas P. Farley** (Hearst Books, 2005)

Posterity: Letters of Great Americans to their Children by **Dorie McCullough Lawson** (Doubleday, 2004)

Social Graces: Words of Wisdom on Civility in a Changing Society, edited by **Jim Brosseau** (Hearst Books, 2002)

You're Too Kind: A Brief History of Flattery by **Richard Stengel** (Simon & Schuster, 2000)

About the Author

Christie Matheson is a writer whose work has appeared in *Martha Stewart's Body + Soul, Glamour, Shape, Boston, San Francisco, Yoga Journal,* and *The Boston Globe Magazine.* She is the author of *Green Chic: Saving the Earth in Style* and coauthor of *Wine Mondays: Simple Wine Pairings with Seasonal Menus, The Confetti Cakes Cookbook, Confetti Cakes for Kids,* and *Tea Party.* She lives in San Francisco, California and Boston, Massachusetts.